Falling Toward Grace

Falling Toward Grace

Images of Religion and Culture from the Heartland

Edited by

J. KENT CALDER
SUSAN NEVILLE

Photography edited by
KIM CHARLES FERRILL

Copublished by
THE POLIS CENTER AND INDIANA UNIVERSITY PRESS

Library of Congress Cataloging-in-Publication Data

Falling toward grace: images of religion and culture in Indianapolis

/edited by J. Kent Calder, Susan Neville : photography edited by

Kim Charles Ferrill.

p.   cm.

ISBN 0-253-33453-5 (cloth : alk. paper)

1. Indianapolis (Ind.)—Religion—20th century—Miscellanea.

I. Calder, J. Kent. II. Neville, Susan.

BL2527.I6F35 1998

200' .9772'5209049—dc21   98-4045

Copublished by

The Polis Center,
Indiana University-Purdue University
at Indianapolis, as part of the Project on Religion and Urban Culture
with support from Lilly Endowment, Inc.

and
Indiana University Press,
Bloomington and Indianapolis

"Birthday Poem," from *The Essential Etheridge Knight*, by Etheridge Knight, © 1986. Reprinted by permission of University of Pittsburgh Press.

"Sacred Space in Ordinary Time," by Susan Neville first appeared in *Traces of Indiana and Midwestern History,* vol. 8, no.1, winter 1996.

"The Blood Tie," from *Returning*, by Dan Wakefield, appears courtesy of Dan Wakefield and Beacon Press.

Poems by Yusef Komunyakaa are reprinted by permission of Wesleyan University Press.

Contents

Skinny Bow Ties

J. Kent Calder

In the 1950s and through most of the '60s, my family seldom missed a Sunday at church, and my mother made sure my brother, two sisters, and I dressed well for the occasions. My older sister has a snapshot of three of us (our little sister was not yet born) dressed in our Easter finery. At ten years old, she towers above five-year-old me and my three-year-old brother. She is wearing a suit that consists of an ankle-length skirt, a jacket, and a matching hat that ties with a ribbon beneath her chin. She looks very grown up. My brother and I sport new white sport coats, skinny clip-on bow ties, and two-toned black-and-white shoes. My brother's grin has broken into the laugh that got me into trouble during so many church services when we were kids. We appear to be a happy family, basking in the glowing ascendancy of the mainline churches.

By the early 1970s, we had all left the church for one reason or another. The ideas it represented seemed in those days as outdated as the clothes we wore in that snapshot. Whatever the trials we faced as we grew to hard-won maturity, we never looked to organized religion for support. Only as we began to raise our own children and as our own mortalities took shape on the horizon did we come to value our churchgoing past and appreciate the tradition that we had inherited. At least we had something to rebel against and something against which to measure the ideas and personas we were continually trying on. After a good deal of soul-searching and intellectual resistance, I decided that my children deserved as much.

My experience, of course, is not unique. As my baby-boomer generation rounds the third turn in its race to the finish, we consume spirituality in the same manner that in the past we consumed baby food, blue jeans, and diet colas. After looking to politics, sex, or money to fulfill our spiritual needs, we now are coming back to religion. We are Holy Rollers, and we are Catholics; we are Buddhists, Baptists, and Jews; we are likely to follow a charismatic leader to a fiery death amidst a hail of bullets, or we might be led gently into that good night by a maniac who tells us that a spaceship will carry us away. We plan our vacations around visits to religious sites, and we buy books that will help us use the Bible to figure out the stock market. We are in many ways as lost as the conservative critics in our midst portray us, but we are also not afraid to ask questions, and in the end we are likely to find our way, though it may not be the easiest one or the one that is expected.

If we do find our way, the editors of this volume believe that it will be in no small part because of the work of our writers. When John Updike came to Indianapolis in November 1996 to speak, along with Dan Wakefield and Kurt Vonnegut Jr., on the topic of spirit and place, he said that the profession of writing "demands that the writer see the human adventure as something more than a chemical event." What we asked the writers, as well as the photographers, in this volume to do is focus directly on this "something more," especially as it pertains to a particular midwestern city and the end of this particular century. It was a difficult assignment, and the responses are as varied as the perspectives of the contributors. Some grew up here and never left; some live elsewhere but devote their writing to midwestern themes; some are here only temporarily and perceive the strange that lies behind the apparently mundane; and some have come here to stay, but forever feel the pull of other places.

I once heard a Russian émigré who had been educated in the United States and who was returning to his homeland to start a business after the fall of communism speak about how places compete for souls. Though he had lived in America many more years than he had in Russia and though his intellectual framework was Western, his return was necessary and inevitable. This unruly entity, the soul, will have its way, and its attractions and repulsions are what we consider here.

The germ of this project lay in a meeting in the summer of 1995 in which I introduced writer Susan Neville to photographer Kim Charles Ferrill for the purpose of matching Susan's words to Kim's pictures for a feature in the magazine *Traces*, which I edit for the Indiana Historical Society. The haunting meditation, "Sacred Space in Ordinary Time," appeared in the winter 1996 issue of the magazine and fittingly anchors this volume. Not long afterward, David J. Bodenhamer, director of The Polis Center, proposed that the three of us edit a collection of writing and photography on the subject of the sacred in Indianapolis as a part of The Polis Center's multifaceted project on Religion and Urban Culture, funded by the Lilly Endowment, Inc.

As articulated by Bodenhamer, the central goal of that project "is to nurture public inquiry and civic conversation about the role of religion in the creation and re-creation of urban community in one American city, Indianapolis, and, by implication, in other American cities." It was Bodenhamer's inspiration to include in this large project—among the voices of the city's academic, religious, and cultural institutions and its neighborhood and community organizations—the perspectives of writers and photographers. For that the editors of this volume are grateful. Indiana has at times been known as a place where the opinions of writers and artists mattered, and in making a place for them in this project The Polis Center extends and strengthens that tradition.

In his spiritual autobiography *Sartor Resartus (The Tailor Retailored*, 1836), Thomas Carlyle indicted the materialism of his age through the expansive metaphor of clothing. Anything that kept people from looking below the surface of things, that discouraged them from innovation or experimentation constituted "Clothing." Tradition, or "Custom," was one kind of clothing. "Am I to view the Stupendous with stupid indifference," he asked, "because I have seen it twice, or two-hundred, or two-million times?" Tradition, through familiar associations, can mask the wonder and the terror of existence, but it can also provide solace and protection when that wonder and terror threaten to destroy. This is the predicament of my generation, and, in another way, it is the predicament of the midwestern city in which I live. Having abandoned tradition to see the world new, my generation now moves in the direction of tradition in order to save ourselves and our children from chaos. Our hope is that by closely examining our traditions, we will not be misled. Indianapolis, on the other hand, is a place where tradition has never been easily abandoned and where the intellectual atmosphere has at times, as evidenced by the writings of Wakefield and Vonnegut, verged on the claustrophobic. The city that is revealed here, however, is one where differences abound and where experimentation, if not always encouraged, is at least possible.

As I examine the forty-year-old photograph of my siblings and me, I wonder if our smiles derive from anything other than our pleasure in our new clothes. I doubt the grins would be so big if we were looking much below the surface of things. Nevertheless, I remember those days fondly—the church suppers, Christmas parties, Ping-Pong tournaments, Sunday-school classes, and people genuinely concerned about my soul—and I make a note to try to find for my wardrobe one of those skinny bow ties.

2

Passport to the Other
Kim Charles Ferrill

As a young boy I helped my father build small shacks for migrant farm workers. My father had worked the fields with them for a summer before taking up the carpentry trade. He knew about the shacks. He built good ones.

The shacks were later torn down, and the fields of tomatoes gave way to corn and soybeans. I never got the chance to meet the migrant workers. For years they came and went and I didn't see them. I felt as though I had missed something.

As a documentary photographer I work on projects that take me into places and experiences that I would not normally get to see. When the chance to photograph an event in the Hispanic community arose, I eagerly scheduled it. Therefore it was with much anticipation that I arrived at St. Patrick's a full half hour before the scheduled start of the Fiesta of Our Lady of Guadalupe. I took the first space in the corner of the parking lot, which placed me close to the front door so I could leave when I wanted. I had been told that a mariachi band would be performing at the fiesta, but other than that I didn't have a clue as to what would happen, so I readied my cameras and placed extra film in my camera bag.

Fifteen minutes after I took my prime parking space a Ford Econoline van with Mexican plates pulled into the parking lot. It had a row of small balls strung across the top of the front window and a Mexican hat on the dashboard. The mariachi band, it turned out, was from Mexico. There aren't any local ones. Another van soon followed, and the occupants of both spilled out onto the streets of Fountain Square and began warming up their instruments and voices. They were dressed in black outfits with silver concho-like buttons running the full length of their pantlegs.

An hour after the fiesta had begun people were still arriving. The church was crowded, and many people were standing in the aisles and entryway. Most of the people came in family groups. Grandparents, parents, and children gathered in the entryway before sitting as a family in the church. The feeling of family unity was a tangible presence. Many of the young people were dressed in traditional garb, and some of the señoritas carried roses that were lit by small battery-powered lights.

One of the main attractions of the Fiesta of Our Lady of Guadalupe is a procession through the church that winds its way around the interior of the church and then up to the front where a large figure of Our Lady of Guadalupe hangs on the wall. Candles and flowers surrounded the figure, and colored lights flooded the Our Lady figure and the Mexican flag above it. The robes of the figure seemed to be glowing.

The trumpets of the mariachi band began blowing at a predetermined time during the mass, and all the band members played loudly as the procession moved over its prescribed route and helpers with baskets on long poles collected money from the congregation. The band, which led the procession, then serenaded the Lady with their music. The trumpets were the loudest thing I had ever heard within the confines of a church. Each of the band members took turns singing into a

4

microphone, and at the end of the verse all the members of the band added their voices to the soloist's lamentations. In Spanish it was perfect. It could never have sounded so sincerely plaintive in English.

After the first procession of the evening I went outside the church to cool off, and I saw that people had parked in all the spaces of the lot, all the lanes in the lot, and had spilled out into the streets around the church. By my count I would have had to move six cars to free mine. This was not an Anglo parking plan. It looked like parking I had seen in small villages in New Mexico, and perhaps it was village parking, only Indianapolis style.

In retrospect my failed plan for an early departure was a blessing. I returned to the church and just watched people. Watching them for over three hours that night I noticed things about their faces that provided quite an awakening for me. I saw the features of young Aztec warriors; I saw faces of high-mountain Indians in Peru. I saw features that I had only seen on the Discovery Channel.

Sitting there for three hours, remembering only tiny remnants of high-school Spanish, surrounded by colors from a palette I was unaccustomed to and music that I had only heard from the speakers in Mexican restaurants, I felt lost. I was a stranger among this community. I felt as though I had wandered into a church in a foreign country. Indianapolis felt very far away that night, yet I knew all along it was just outside.

The evening started to wind down and people started to leave and still I sat there, soaking up the experience, trying to memorize the faces. Before this night the Hispanic population of Indianapolis had practically been invisible to me, but never again will I pass these faces and not see them. I have been awakened to their presence and been granted a peek at their spirit.

I sat in the last row of pews and tried to put the evening into perspective. I remembered how early on in my photography career I had studied photojournalism. I was never without my camera. I was ready to "snap," "take," or "capture" images at any given moment. It was an aggressive posture that I shed early on, and it gave me grave doubts as to my future. As I matured as a photographer I came to understand that what I was looking for, the "other" in our world, would come to me only if I paid it quiet attention.

Photography has become, for me, a way of living. It is, as photographer Minor White has summed up, "photography for what it is, and for what else it is," a sentiment that clearly covers all participants in this book.

I stood outside of St. Patrick's that night and watched the last car leave. My earlier parking plans seemed funny now, and I smiled as the car I was watching honked a horn and as the familiar tune of "La Cucarracha" blared from under its hood. I walked back to my car, and I thought of the migrant workers of my youth. Tonight the exotic people I had dreamed about as a boy came and went, and I had taken a good, long look. And I was right all those years ago. I had been missing out.

As I walked to my car the silence seemed odd. The city had swallowed the people and the sounds that they made as if they had never been there. I drove out of the city and into the country I knew so well. I drove in the dark past the fields where my father and I had built the shacks so many years ago, and I wondered what my father would have thought of this night and of the small boy who finally got his wish.

Falling toward Grace
Susan Neville

They heard the sound of the Lord God walking in the garden at the time of the evening breeze.
—Genesis 3

The roof of the produce stand is corrugated plastic, and the light that filters through has the green translucency of a leaf. There are no side walls, only a wooden floor and some wooden beams, and the warm smell of tomato and melon.

A young man chews on an uncooked snap bean and unloads a box of sweet corn from a pickup truck. The bean is sweet, he says, the corn, the fruit, the air is sweet. There's a breeze caught and channeled by the roof, so it feels, underneath it, like an oceanside gazebo.

And through and over everything the green light, that phosphorescent yellow-green you see hovering eight inches or so above spring-fed pools, a light you could willingly drown in.

This is the best job I've ever had, a young woman says; it's heaven here. She looks at the boy at the cash register when she says this. How could he not be in love with her? She stands there stacking galaxies of smooth-skinned apples and black plums. You know, she says, if you look closely, there are white stars in the skin of purple fruit, and flames inside a strawberry.

Look closely. This is how she wants her life to feel always, every minute of every day and every day of every year and infinitely beyond years. We could all be happy here, she thinks, each one of us held inside the green wind like separate seeds inside one ripe fruit.

If Henry James was right, and "the whole concern of both morality and religion is with the matter of our acceptance of the universe," then this feeling is a religious one. For one moment, this girl accepts it here, all of it.

But it's already mid-August and the tomatoes are beginning to rot too quickly. Why would anyone take this produce home? It won't even last the afternoon.

It is of course a fallen world, but after work she won't so much fall as leap down from the wooden floor and onto a concrete parking lot, holding paper bags full of end-of-season southern peaches and red potatoes, surrounded now by cranky cars and dust from new construction and an abandoned strip mall that was built to be ephemeral. An unfiltered, too-white sun reminds her of her many unrepented sins. Up above her head there's a robot taking tourist shots on the dusty red planet of Mars. The unspoken fear? That somewhere in all that dust is evidence that there were at one time sentient beings, and it used to be a garden.

As this place was, or so we're told.

I've been thinking a lot about Eden. Perhaps because I've been reading the words in this collection, and thinking about them in the context of Indiana literature. The story of the Fall is one that Midwestern writers tell again and again. Perhaps because this literally was a garden of hardwood forests, "One great big woods," Oliver Johnson wrote of this place in *A Home in the Woods*, "miles and miles in every direction." Yet less than one hundred years later, Booth Tarkington would write that Indianapolis because of its "mania for factories," the snake in the nineteenth century garden, had grown " dirty with an incredible completeness."

And perhaps I've been thinking about Eden because the story is an end-of-an-era story, a story for the turn of a millennium. The Golden Age in Indiana literature, in itself a lost Eden about lost Edens, was a turn-of-the-century age, with turn-of-the-century concerns, particularly an ambivalence about the future: a nostalgia for a more perfect past as well as an at times explicit wish for the new world to explode into this one, if necessary, with a cleansing violence that would burn away the evil present. Or lift us all above it. A revival or a rapture; you can take your pick. A revival or a rapture or, depending on your taste, perhaps an angel or flying saucer—something to usher us safely across to the new world on the other side of the century's turning.

This collection of words and images has been an attempt to see a specific place, Indianapolis, as it tells the story of this particular time. And while the story we're telling is still, in many ways, the story of Adam and Eve hovering in the "halflight," as Marianne Boruch calls it, between two worlds, the image of the earth as garden has been replaced by the image of a fragile blue cell floating in a brooding, silent universe.

It's fitting that many of these essays touched on silence and sound as artists try to tune into the frequency of the music of the spheres. Some of them listened in churches and synagogues and mosques, and some outside of them. Some heard something humming through the silence, and some heard nothing at all.

One thing photographers and writers hold in common is the the need to pay attention. Look closely, the girl said as she stacked those plums. Listen closely. She somehow knew that in the attention itself there is, if not a fall back into grace, at least that fall toward it.

7

SUNDAY'S TURNING
Alice Friman

By the end of June
our Japanese Maple begins to turn,
slow as a girl in a full-length mirror
trying to catch the moment
when one color swirls into the next—
the iridescent change precipitated in her face
swung open in her skirts at last.

Sunday in Indiana, hump
of the year's turning, we hack
and weed, flail at a wild mulberry
that roars over our backyard fence
like the nine-headed Hydra. We chop,
throttle, stomp it down. By tomorrow
we'll call ourselves Heracles,
our scratches *Purple Hearts*, our victory—
or is it defeat—waiting for pick-up,
shriveled in ropes at the curb.

Later we'll walk our usual,
down Central to 54th, pause on the steps
of The Immaculate Heart of Mary
to rest my bum leg or retie a shoe
just when dusk, that peculiar time of turning,
clusters around each streetlight, uneasy
as shadow or the body around its star.

SILENCE

Scott Russell Sanders

Finding a traditional Quaker meeting in Indianapolis would not be easy. No steeple would loom above the meeting house, no bell tower, no neon cross. No billboard out front would name the preacher or proclaim the sermon topic or tell sinners how to save their souls. No crowd of nattily dressed churchgoers would stream toward the entrance from a vast parking lot filled with late-model cars. No bleat and moan of organ would roll from the sanctuary doors.

I knew all of that from having worshipped with Quakers off and on for thirty years, beginning when I was a graduate student in England. They are a people who call so little attention to themselves or their gathering places as to be nearly invisible. Yet when I happened to be in Indianapolis one Sunday this past January, I still set out in search of the meeting house without street address or map. My search was not made any easier by the snow billowing down on the city that morning. I recalled hearing that the North Meadow Circle of Friends gathers in a house near the intersection of Meridian and 16th Streets, a spot I found easily enough. Although I could not miss the imposing Catholic Center nearby on Meridian nor the Joy of All Who Sorrow Eastern Orthodox Church just a block away on 16th, the only landmark at the intersection itself was the International House of Pancakes. Figuring somebody in there might be able to direct me to the Quakers, I went inside, where I was greeted by the smell of sausage and the frazzled gaze of the hostess. No, she'd never heard of any Quakers.

"But there's the phone book," she told me, gesturing with a sheaf of menus. "You're welcome to look them up." I thanked her, and started with the yellow pages. No luck under "Churches." Nothing under "Religion." Nothing under "Quakers" or "Friends, Society of." Finally, in the white pages, I found a listing for the North Meadow Circle, with a street address just a couple of blocks away. As I returned the phone book to its cubbyhole, I glanced across the room, where a throng of diners tucked into heaping platters of food, and I saw through the plate-glass window a man slouching past on the sidewalk. He wore a knit hat encrusted with leaves, a jacket torn at the elbows to reveal several dingy layers of cloth underneath, baggy trousers held up with a belt of rope, and broken leather shoes wrapped with silver duct tape. His face was the color of dust. He carried a bulging gray sack over his shoulder, like a grim Santa Claus. Pausing at a trash can, he bent down to retrieve something, stuffed the prize in his bag, then shuffled north on Meridian into the slant of snow.

I thought how odd it was that none of the diners rushed out to drag him from the street into the House of Pancakes for a hot meal. Then again, I didn't rush out either. I only stood there feeling pangs of guilt, an ache as familiar as heartburn. What held me back? Wouldn't the Jesus whom I try to follow in my own muddled way have chosen to feed that man instead of searching for a prayer meeting? I puzzled over this as I drove the few blocks to Talbott Street, on the lookout for number 1710, the address I had turned up in the phone book. The root of all my reasons for neglecting that homeless man, I decided, was fear. He might be crazy, might be strung out, might be dangerous. He would almost certainly have problems greater than I could solve. And there were so many more like him, huddled out front of missions or curled up in doorways all over Indianapolis this bitterly cold morning. If I fed one person, why not two? Why not twenty? Once I acknowledged the human need rising around me, what would keep me from drowning in all that hurt?

A whirl of guilt and snow blinded me to number 1710, even though I cruised up and down that stretch of Talbot Street three times. I did notice that the neighborhood was in transition, with some houses boarded up and others newly spiffed up. A few of the homes were small enough for single families, but most were big frame duplexes trimmed in fretwork and painted in pastels, or low brick apartment buildings that looked damp and dark and cheap. On my third pass along Talbott I saw a portly man with a bundle of papers clamped under one arm turning in at the gate of a gray clapboard house. I rolled down my window to ask if he knew where the Friends worshipped, and he answered with a smile, "Right here."

I parked next door in a lot belonging to the Herron School of Art. As I climbed out of the car, a pinwheel of pigeons lifted from the roof of the school and spun across the sky, a swirl of silver against pewter clouds. No artists appeared to be up and about this early on a Sunday, but some of their handiwork was on display in the yard, including a flutter of cloth strips dangling from wire strung between posts, an affair that looked, under the weight of snow, like bedraggled laundry. An inch or two of snow covered the parking lot, and more was falling. Footprints scuffled away from the five or six cars, converged on the sidewalk, then led up to the gate where I had seen the man carrying the bundle of papers. True to form, the Quakers had mounted no

sign on the brick gateposts, none on the iron fence, none on the lawn. Twin wreathes tied with red ribbons flanked the porch, and a wind-chime swayed over the front steps. Only when I climbed onto the porch did I see a small painted board next to the door, announcing that an "Unprogrammed (Silent) Meeting" is held here every First Day at 10 a.m., and that "Each person's presence is reason to celebrate."

There was celebration in the face of the woman who greeted me at the door. "So good to see you," she whispered. "Have you worshipped with Quakers before?" I answered with a nod. "Wonderful," she murmured, pointing the way: "We're right in there."

I walked over creaking floorboards from the narrow entrance hall into a living room cluttered with bookshelves, cozy chairs, and exuberant plants. Stacks of pamphlets filled the mantle above a red brick fireplace. Posters on the walls proclaimed various Quaker testimonies, including opposition to the death penalty and a vow against war. It was altogether a busy, frowzy, good-natured space.

From there I entered the former dining room, which had become the meeting room, and I took my seat on a wooden bench near the bay windows. Five other benches were ranged about, facing one another, to form an open square. Before closing my eyes, I noticed that I was the ninth person to arrive. No one spoke. For a long while the only sounds were the scritch of floorboards announcing latecomers, the sniffles and coughs from winter colds, the rumble and whoosh of the furnace, the calling of doves and finches from the eaves. The silence grew so deep that I could hear the blood beating in my ears. I tensed the muscles in my legs, balled up my fists, then let them relax. I tried stilling my thoughts, tried hushing my own inward monologue, in hopes of hearing the voice of God.

That brazen expectation, which grips me now and again, is a steady article of faith for Quakers. They recite no creed, and they have little use for theology, but they do believe that every person may experience direct contact with God. They also believe we are most likely to achieve that contact in stillness, either alone or in the gathered meeting, which is why they use no ministers or music, no readings or formal prayers, no script at all, but merely wait in silence for inward promptings. Quakers are mystics, in other words, but homely and practical ones, less concerned with escaping to heaven than with living responsibly on earth. The pattern was set in the seventeenth century by their founder, George Fox, who journeyed around England amid civil and ecclesiastical wars, searching for true religion. He did not find it in cathedrals or churches, did not hear it from the lips of priests, did not discover it in art or books. Near despair, he finally encountered what he was seeking within his own depths: "When all my hopes in all men were gone, so that I had nothing outwardly to help me, nor could I tell what to do, then, oh then, I heard a voice which said, 'There is one, even Christ Jesus that can speak to thy condition,' and when I heard it my heart did leap for joy."

My heart was too heavy for leaping, weighed down by thoughts of the unmet miseries all around me. The homeless man shuffled past the House of Pancakes with his trash bag, right down the main street of my brain. I leaned forward on the bench, elbows on knees, listening. By and by there came a flurry of sirens from Meridian, and the sudden ruckus made me twitch. I opened my eyes and took in more of the room. There were twelve of us now, eight women and four men, ranging in age from twenty or so to upwards of seventy. No suits or ties, no skirts, no lipstick or mascara. Instead of dress-up clothes, the Friends wore sweaters or wool shirts in earth colors, jeans or corduroys, boots

or running shoes or sandals with wool socks. The wooden benches, buffed and scarred from long use, were cushionless except for a few rectangular scraps of carpet, only one of which had been claimed. A pair of toy metal cars lay nose-to-nose on one bench, a baby's bib and a Bible lay on another, and here and there lay boxes of Kleenex. Except for those few objects and the benches and people, the room was bare. There was no crucifix hanging on the walls, no saint's portrait, no tapestry, no decoration whatsoever. The only relief from the white paint were three raised-panel doors that led into closets or other rooms. The only movement, aside from an occasional shifting of hands or legs, was the sashay of lace curtains beside the bay windows when the furnace blew, and those windows also provided the only light.

To anyone glancing in from outside, we would have offered a dull spectacle: a dozen grown people sitting on benches, hands clasped or lying open on knees, eyes closed, bodies upright or hunched over, utterly quiet. "And your strength is, to stand still," Fox wrote in one of his epistles, "that ye may receive refreshings; that ye may know, how to wait, and how to walk before God, by the Spirit of God within you." When the refreshing comes, when the Spirit stirs within, one is supposed to rise in the meeting and proclaim what God has whispered or roared. It might be a prayer, a few lines from the Bible or another holy book, a testimony about suffering in the world, a moral concern, or a vision. If the words are truly spoken, they are understood to flow not from the person but from the divine source that upholds and unites all of Creation.

In the early days, when hundreds and then thousands of people harkened to the message of George Fox as he traveled through England, there was often so much fervent speaking in the meetings for worship, so much shaking and shouting under the pressure of Spirit, that hostile observers mocked these trembling Christians by calling them "Quakers." The humble followers of Fox, indifferent to the world's judgment, accepted the name. They also called themselves Seekers, Children of the Light, Friends in the Truth, and, eventually, the Society of Friends. Most of these names, along with much of their religious philosophy, derived from the Gospel according to John. There in the first chapter of the recently-translated King James version they could read that Jesus "was the true Light, which lighteth every man that cometh into the world." In the fifteenth chapter they could read Christ's assurance to his followers: "Henceforth I call you not servants; for the servant knoweth not what his lord doeth: but I have called you friends; for all things that I have heard of my Father I have made known unto you."

There was no outward sign of fervor on the morning of my visit to the North Meadow Circle of Friends. I sneezed once, and that was the loudest noise in the room for a long while. In the early years, meetings might go on for half a day, but in our less patient era they usually last about an hour. There is no set ending time. Instead, one of the elders, sensing when the silence has done its work, will signal the conclusion by shaking hands with a neighbor. Without looking at my watch, I guessed that most of an hour had passed, and still no one had spoken.

It would have been rare in Fox's day for an entire meeting to pass without any vocal ministry, as the Quakers call it. But it is not at all rare in our own time, judging from my reading and from my visits to meetings around the country. Indeed, Quaker historians acknowledge that over the past three centuries the Society has experienced a gradual decline in spiritual energy, broken by occasional periods of revival, and graced by many vigorous, God-centered individuals. Quakerism itself arose in reaction to a lackluster Church of England, just as the Protestant Reformation challenged a corrupt and listless Catholic Church, just as Jesus challenged the hidebound Judaism of his day. It seems to be the fate of religious movements to lose energy over time, as direct encounters with the Spirit give way to secondhand rituals and creeds, as prophets give way to priests, as living insight hardens into words and glass and stone.

The Quakers have resisted this fate better than most, but they have not escaped it entirely. Last century, when groups of disgruntled Friends despaired of reviving what they took to be a moribund Society, they split off to form congregations that would eventually hire ministers, sing hymns, read scriptures aloud, and behave for all the world like other low-temperature Protestant churches. In Midwestern states such as Indiana, in fact, these so-called "programmed" Quaker churches have come to outnumber the traditional silent meetings.

I could have gone to a Friends' Church in Indianapolis that Sunday morning, but I was in no mood to sit through anybody's program, no matter how artful or uplifting it might be. What I craved was silence—not absolute silence, for I welcomed the ruckus of doves and finches, but rather the absence of human noise. I spend nearly all of my waking hours immersed in language, bound to machines, following streets, obeying schedules, seeing and hearing and touching only what my clever species has made. I often yearn, as I did that morning, to withdraw from all our schemes and formulas, to escape from the obsessive human story, to slip out of my own small self and meet the great Self, the nameless mystery at the core of being. I had a better chance of doing that here among the silent Quakers, I felt, than anywhere else I might have gone.

A chance is not a guarantee, of course. I had spent hundreds

12

of hours in Quaker meetings over the years, and only rarely had I felt myself dissolved away into the Light. More often, I had sat on hard benches rummaging through my past, counting my breaths, worrying about chores, reciting verses in my head, thinking about the pleasures and evils of the day, half hoping and half fearing that some voice not my own would break through to command my attention. It's no wonder that most religions put on a show, anything to fence in the wandering mind and fence out the terror. It's no wonder that only a dozen people would seek out this Quaker meeting on a Sunday morning, while tens of thousands of people were sitting through scripted performances in other churches across Indianapolis.

Carrying on one's own spiritual search, without maps or guide, can be scary. When I sink into meditation, I often remember the words of Pascal: "The eternal silence of these infinite spaces fills me with dread." What I take him to mean is that the universe is bewilderingly large and enigmatic; it does not speak to us in any clear way; and yet we feel, in our brief spell of life, an urgent desire to learn where we are and why we are and who we are. The silence reminds us that we may well be all on our own in a universe empty of meaning, each of us an accidental bundle of molecules, forever cut off from the truth. If that is roughly what Pascal meant, then I suspect that most people who have thought much about our condition would share his dread. Why else do we surround ourselves with so much noise? We plug in, tune in, cruise around, talk, read, run, as though determined to drown out the terrifying silence of those infinite spaces.

A car in need of a muffler roared down Talbott Street past the meeting house, and the racket hauled me back to the surface of my mind. Only when I surfaced did I realize how far down I had dived. Had I touched bottom? Was there a bottom at all, and if so, was it only the floor of my private psyche, or was it the ground of being?

As I pondered, someone stood up heavily from a bench across the room from me. Although Quakers are not supposed to care who speaks, I opened my eyes, squinting against the somber snowlight. The one standing was the portly man whom I had asked the way to the meeting house. A ruff of pearl-gray hair fell to his shoulders, a row of pens weighted the breast pocket of his shirt, and the cuffs of his jeans were neatly rolled. He cleared his throat. In times of prayer, he said, he often feels overwhelmed by a sense of the violence and cruelty and waste in the world. Everywhere he looks, he sees more grief. When he complains to God that he's fed up with problems and would like some solutions for a change, God answers that the solutions are for humans to devise. If we make our best effort, God will help. But God isn't going to do the work for us. We're called not to save the world but to carry on the work of love.

All of this was said intimately, affectionately, in the tone of a person reporting a conversation with a close friend. Having uttered his few words, the speaker sat down. The silence flowed back over us. A few minutes later, he grasped the hand of the woman sitting next to him, and with a rustle of limbs greetings were exchanged all around the room. We blinked at one another, returned from wherever it was we had gone together, separated once more into our twelve bodies. Refreshed, I took up the sack of my self, which seemed lighter than when I had carried it into this room. I looked about, gazing with tenderness at each face, even though I was a stranger to all of them.

A guest book was passed around for signatures. The only visitor besides myself was a man freshly arrived from Louisiana,

13

who laughed about needing to buy a heavier coat for this Yankee weather. An elder mentioned that donations could be placed in a small box on the mantle, if anyone felt moved to contribute. People rose to announce social concerns and upcoming events. After an hour and a half of nearly unbroken silence, suddenly the air filled with talk. It was as though someone had released into our midst an aviary's worth of birds.

Following their custom, the Friends took turns introducing themselves and recounting some noteworthy event from the past week. A woman told about lunching with her daughter-in-law, trying to overcome some hard feelings, and about spilling a milk-shake in the midst of the meal. A man told how his son's high school basketball coach took the boy out of a game for being too polite toward the opponents. The father jokingly advised his son to scowl and threaten, like the professional athletes whom the coach evidently wished for him to emulate. This prompted a woman to remark that her colleagues at work sometimes complained that she was too honest: "Lie a little, they tell me. It greases the wheels." The only student in the group, a young woman with a face as clear as spring water, told of an assignment that required her to write about losing a friend. "And I've spent the whole week in memory," she said. A man reported on his children's troubled move to a new school. A woman told of her conversation with a prisoner on death-row. Another told of meeting with a union organizer while visiting Mexico. "They're so poor," she said, "we can't even imagine how poor." A woman explained that she and her husband, who cared nothing for football, would watch the Super Bowl that afternoon, because the husband's estranged son from an earlier marriage was playing for the Green Bay Packers. When my turn came, I described hiking one afternoon that week with my daughter Eva, how we studied the snow

for animal tracks, how her voice lit up the woods. Others spoke about cleaning house, going to a concert, losing a job, caring for grandchildren, suffering pain, hearing a crucial story: small griefs, small celebrations.

After all twelve of us had spoken, we sat for one final moment in silence, to mark an end to our time together. Then we rose from those unforgiving benches, pulled on coats, and said our good-byes. On my way to the door, I was approached by several Friends who urged me to come again, and I thanked them for their company.

As I walked outside into the sharp wind, I recalled how George Fox had urged his followers to "walk cheerfully over the world, answering that of God in every one." There were still no footprints leading to the doors of the art school, no lights burning in the studios. I brushed snow from the windows of my car with gloved hands. To go home, I should have turned south on Meridian, but instead I turned north. I drove slowly, peering into alleys and doorways, looking for the man in the torn jacket with the bulging gray sack over his shoulder. I never saw him, and I did not know what I would have done if I had seen him. Give him a few dollars? Offer him a meal at the International House of Pancakes? Take him home?

Eventually I turned around and headed south, right through the heart of Indianapolis. In spite of the snow, traffic was picking up, for the stores recognized no Sabbath. I thought of the eighteenth-century Quaker, John Woolman, who gave up shop-keeping and worked modestly as a tailor, so that he would have time for seeking and serving God. "So great is the hurry in the spirit of this world," he wrote in 1772, "that in aiming to do business quickly and to gain wealth the creation at this day doth loudly groan." In my Quakerly mood, much of what I saw in the capital was distressing—the trash on the curbs, the bars and girlie clubs, the war memorials, the sheer weight of buildings, the smear of pavement, the shop windows filled with trinkets, the homeless men and women plodding along through the snow, the endless ads. I had forgotten that today was Super Bowl Sunday until the woman at meeting spoke of it, and now I could see that half the billboards and marquees and window displays in the city referred to this national festival, a day set aside for devotion by more people, and with more fervor, than any date on the Christian calendar.

"The whole mechanism of modern life is geared for a flight from God," wrote Thomas Merton. I have certainly found it so. The hectic activity imposed on us by jobs and families and avocations and amusements, the accelerating pace of technology, the flood of information, the proliferation of noise, all combine to keep us from that inward stillness where meaning is to be found. How can we grasp the nature of things, how can we lead gathered lives, if we are forever dashing about like water-striders on the moving surface of a creek?

By the time I reached the highway outside of Indianapolis, snow was falling steadily and blowing lustily, whiting out the way ahead. Headlights did no good. I should have pulled over until the sky cleared, like a sensible fellow. But the snow held me. I lost all sense of motion, lost awareness of road and car. I seemed to be floating in the whirl of flakes, caught up in silence, alone yet not alone, as though I had slipped by accident into the state that a medieval mystic had called the cloud of unknowing. Memory fled, words flew away, and there was only the brightness, here and everywhere.

15

16

Friends Meeting Space, TALBOT STREET

17

Carmelite Monastery, **COLD SPRING ROAD**

18

United Methodist Church, MERIDIAN STREET

Greater Faith Apostolic Church, CENTRAL AVENUE

19

Jesus In The Arms of The Blessed Virgin, ST. JOHN'S

St. John's Catholic Church, DETAIL

20

Sts. Peter & Paul Catholic Church

Christ Mission Baptist Church

St. John's Catholic Church, **ROOF DETAIL**

Holy Temple of God, **WINTHROP AVENUE**

SEASONS OF THE SPIRIT
Jeanette Vanausdall

In my dream we live on the water. I don't know what water or where. It doesn't matter. It is somewhere where the outdoors is, all year long, extra living space. It is a house like a villa on the Aegean, open to the sea, where I waft like a breeze under an arch, through a courtyard and into sunlight. In the dream I am crying because we are returning to the Midwest for some reason. I keep burying my face in my husband's shoulder and saying I can't, I can't into a summerweight navy blazer. Does he even have a navy blazer and why is he wearing it now? It's probably something about why we're going back, something about careers and responsibility and dry cleaners and industrial parks and strip malls. Whole weeks when I barely get out of my mini van. But for the moment I am wearing a gauzy cotton dress that coils around my bare legs.

My friend has a clear retirement plan. He wants to end his days as an eccentric old gringo somewhere where everyone speaks Spanish and you never have to wear socks. To that end he is studying conversational Spanish. This seems as sensible to me as a 401(k).

The problem is that we live in a place where too many months of the year we huddle indoors, dart from shelter to vehicle trying to avoid as much of the outside as we possibly can. This is the urban Midwest. We do not experience Yellowstone winters here, deep virginal snows that lie undefiled a whole season. The hot breath of a lone buffalo suspended in the bright, brittle air. These are not the winters of watercolor landscapes and environmental Christmas cards.

Here, after a particularly brutal winter the streets are lined with oily snow, so packed and icy it will still be here in April. And utterly, utterly gray. My car is filthy. The house is littered with drying gloves, hats and boots in various stages of rigor mortis. Last week's snowmen looking like death camp survivors. The thaw, when it finally comes, will reveal all manner of plastic bags, lost mittens, sheets of sodden newsprint, entire pizza boxes, the detritus of a whole season abandoned to the elements. We give up here about mid-January.

Here we battle winter illnesses as if they were entities. On a wet October night my seven year old says, "My throat's kind of itchy," and in her one plaintive statement I hear my sentence. I will be nursing both children, and myself, from now until May. I will see my pediatrician more often than I see my husband.

I know no truly happy people when winter comes to this city. Our spiritual selves curl up like green leaves with the first real frost. We kick into the survival mode and survivors, by and large, have little energy for spiritual reflection, for praise or thanksgiving. It is the dark night of the soul, the hibernation of our better selves. "Awful darkness," Edward Lear called it, on "long, long wintry nights."

Winter desolation has been a subject of the myths of most ancient cultures. The myths are more than tales that explain the changing seasons; they are passion plays of death and burial, darkness and grief, and violence to the human psyche. Winters past have been credited with being the source of our puritan forebears' industry and perseverance. Today, psychologists treat a type of seasonal depression which is supposedly caused by a deficit of a certain frequency of light. Diagnosis and therapy are new; the condition is not. "Lord, this is a huge rayn!" Chaucer wrote. "This were a weder for to slepen inne!"

In Indiana, even people who profess to love the snow and cold, usually winter sports enthusiasts, go elsewhere to enjoy it. They head west to ski, because here our snow isn't even suitable for sport. Or it's unreliably so.

We stay at a little place in Clearwater Beach, a mom-and-pop establishment, five units well off the strip and on a lovely quiet little bay. Our proprietress will hug us good-bye when we leave. I sit on her dock one morning and hear her laughing inside her apartment. Eventually she joins me for coffee. "That Howie Mandel," she chuckles. "They're a funny people, don't you think?"

I pretend I don't understand the reference and we chat about what it's like back in Indianapolis at this time of year. She understands my despair because she and her husband used to manage Seven-Elevens in New Jersey. "You know what?" she says. "We've been here eighteen years and I can't remember a day that I've felt depressed."

I'm very quiet, watching her toss pieces of leftover pork roast to the snowy egret that hangs out in their yard. It's waiting on her patio for her every morning. They get pelicans and a blue heron too. I ask her who dominates. "Oh, the heron," she replies quickly. "No question."

"You know what though," she says after awhile. "The one thing... It's a constant battle down here, trying to keep the sand out of your house."

Boo-hoo, I want to say, but I don't because she's just trying to make me feel better. Like that's one thing I don't have to contend with up north! The only thing she can think of.

Midwesterners have favorite stories about their worst winter moments. Mine happened a few years ago when I had a miserable cold and my dog had intestinal problems. She had to go out about every forty minutes all night. It was sleeting and the

wind was as bitter cold as I can ever remember. My nose ran torrents onto my chapped lips, but it was too cold to take my gloves off to do anything about it. There was not another soul awake in our subdivision as we crouched there together, both of us whimpering in the dark.

The problem is we spend so much of our lives in the Midwest waiting to do so many things, anything that requires being outdoors. All winter we are weighed down with clothing. We batten down our hatches, both architectural and psychic, and still we are besieged by viruses. We add pound after pound to bodies in utter torpor. We used to eat, as a species, for extra layers of fat to survive the cold and the increased heart rate that any kind of exertion requires in the winter. We no longer live or work outdoors, and still we compensate. The question is, for what.

A friend in Phoenix, whom I otherwise like, insists that the weather there gets kinda boring.

"I'm sure," I retort. "Like good health. Day after day, the same damn thing."

I am not as spiritually self-contained as some of my friends and neighbors, perhaps. I cannot separate my spiritual self from my environment. Not entirely. I am easily distracted by discomfort, inconvenience, urban malaise.

Even Jesus withdrew to the wilderness to be tested and to triumph. I have seen the Judean wilderness. It is only a few short steps into the desert from the Mount of Olives with its bird's-eye view of Jerusalem. I stepped into it with my back to the city, knowing that I was seeing probably the only thing, with the possible exception of a few paving stones, that Jesus actually saw.

In the Midwest we don't have a landscape that inspires spiritual contemplation. We don't have a desert landscape of solitude and renunciation here. We don't have a mountain land-

23

scape that inspires ascent and aspiration. We don't experience the primal tug of vast bodies of water. The spirituality of the woodlands, if there was one, has all but disappeared and Indianapolis, for all its wonderful attributes as a safe and clean city in which to raise a family etc, etc, is indistinguishable from most other urban centers. Let's face it.

As I write this piece the winter of my discontent has been made glorious summer. My youngest daughter becomes some kind of wild thing when she's outdoors from sun-up to sun-down, a grubby little summer creature with a glint in her eye and a new awareness of her elemental self. She has two skinned knees and is covered with insect bites. On the rare moments when I can catch her as she scurries past, I bury my face in her hair, in that wonderful sweaty child smell. She pushes free and is gone across the green grass. For the moment I am wearing a gauzy cotton dress that coils around my bare legs, and the darkness is hours away.

IN LUCKY DARK: *With the Beech Grove Benedictines*
Patricia Henley

"Pope John XXIII was Pope only ninety days when he announced his surprise plan to convoke the Roman Catholic Church's 21st Ecumenical Council. When the Prelates and the Bishops of the Church assembled in Rome and the Council began on October 11, 1962, the Pontiff was eighty years old. This Council, known as Vatican II, was giftful to the whole human family in many ways. But according to Karl Rahner, one of the greatest theologians of this century, one of the greatest enactments of the Second Vatican Council was the document called Nostra Aetate (October 28, 1965) on the Relationship of the Church to non-Christian religions. In this document, for the first time in history, the Roman Church publicly proclaimed that truth is to be found in other Religions."
— *Sister Pascaline Coff, O.S.B., in her opening address at Gethsemane Encounter 1996*

I

October 27, 1997. A Sunday. The peak of autumn color past, the winter yawning up ahead. I take Interstate 65 South, then the Raymond Street Exit. The Beech Grove houses are neat-as-a-pin Hoosier homes, aluminum sided, vinyl-sided, with maple trees and burning bush still red. It might be 1996 or it might be 1966. Except for the rare satellite dish stuck oddly on the corner of a porch, time passing isn't immediately apparent. Our Lady of Grace Monastery is brick, trimmed in limestone, one of several buildings on forty-three acres given to the Benedictines in the early fifties by Archbishop Shulte of Indianapolis, who dreamed of a home for the aged on the site. That home is there on the corner of Sherman and Southern, the Hermitage. In the center of a circle drive beyond the Hermitage, a stone statue of the Blessed Mother piques my memory.

When I was a girl my school came here—*here*—for a choral event. My father drove me from West Terre Haute. I was an eighth grader at St. Leonard's. It is one of those memories I can't be sure of, can't prove. I just feel it. I think I wore a black gabar-dine skirt, a white cotton blouse and a red nylon scarf as a tie. I remember sitting in the car with my father, feeling nervous. He fiddled with the radio dial, keen to listen to the Cubs game over the static. Thirty-six years later, the foggy memory gives me ease, makes me feel at home.

Inside, the imperative SEEK GOD—gold, two foot high letters—greets everyone who enters. Sister Meg, former prioress and executive director of Monastic Interreligious Dialogue, is an energetic red-headed sprite in her late forties, I assess, wearing simple clothing: a black skirt, a pale rose blouse, Birkenstocks. She gives me a whirlwind tour of the monastery, stopping for a moment in the foyer of the chapel where there hangs a framed photograph of Our Holy Father John Paul II surrounded by religious leaders of other faiths. This photo was taken at the Assisi Peace Conference in 1986, the conference we are commemorating. Tears spring into my eyes; I cannot explain them; this picture of Muslims, Buddhists, Hindus, Greek Orthodox, Anglican, Jews, and others—with the Pope—breaks open my heart.

II

Dr. Norbu, the Dalai Lama's brother, is due later in the day and it will be his first time to attend Catholic Vespers. Sister Meg leaves me in the Monastery library with a stack of papers given last summer at the Gethsemane Encounter at the Abbey of Gethsemane, the Kentucky home of Thomas Merton. The Dalai Lama himself, leader of Tibetan Buddhists, had requested the gathering and was in attendance. I read bits and pieces and finally settle on Sister Pascaline Coff's opening address. Sister Pascaline is a Benedictine from Osage Monastery in Sand Springs, Oklahoma. After she spent a year at a Christian Hindu Ashram in South India, she began the work of interreligious dialogue. As a result of Vatican II, Benedictines were invited by the Vatican to pursue mutual understanding between Christians and non-Christians. The Benedictines and other Catholic monastic orders have taken that call to heart, traveling to Tibet and India, sponsoring the visits of Buddhist nuns and monks in the United States, publishing a newsletter, and spreading the news of East-West understanding whenever the opportunity arises. In the past year articles born of the Buddhist-Christian dialogue have appeared in such mainline Catholic publications as *St. Anthony's Messenger* and *Commonweal*.

III

Not all of the Beech Grove Benedictines meditate. It's a choice. The ones who have taken up the practice gather at 7:30 every morning in the meditation hall to enter into contemplative prayer. The square hall is velvety dim, sparsely furnished along the walls with zabutons—flat, black pillows—topped with zafus, round, ten-inch high cushions traditionally used by Zen Buddhists during meditation. Here and there are low-to-the-floor prayer stools made of wood by a local craftsman. In contemplative prayer, the ancient Christian form of meditation learned from The Cloud of Unknowing, a centuries old book of anonymous authorship, there are few hard and fast rules about how to sit. You may use a chair, a cushion, a stool. Months later, when I would participate in the ten-day Centering Prayer Intensive at Our Lady of Grace, I would pad barefooted into the large meditation room amused at the cheerful nests and stations we built for ourselves over the ten days: participants meditated wrapped in wool blankets and ponchos and afghans, on improvised zafus of folded plaid flannel, on conference chairs. At the end of each eighty-minute sit, the nests remained in the darkened room, sometimes in the ghostly shape of those who had sat and those who would return to sit again, under the crucifix and the photo of a benignly smiling Thomas Merton, the Trappist monk who made one of the initial contacts with Eastern monasticism in 1968. Across the poster: "There is in all things an invisible fecundity, a dimmed light, a meek namelessness, a hidden wholeness."

IV

April, 1972. South Carolina. Spring arrived so early that I had already been to the beach, tanned, drunk gin and tonics. I lived in an apartment complex on the edge of a small college town. My life was about domestic pleasures: admiring my two-year-old's thatch of white-blond hair, the hefty wisteria, learning to drive our red VW bus. A woman friend came to visit, in her tinted aviator glasses, reeking of frangipani. With her she had a book called BE HERE NOW by Ram Dass. A great book, she said. And she left the book with me.

"You may have reasoned and reasoned," Ram Dass wrote, "until you saw the peculiar position that rational man is in & you realize there must be something else, although you have

26

not experienced it. You just infer the presence of 'something else.' It doesn't quite make sense. Nothing 'turns you on.' You haven't experienced it directly but you figured there must be something else, something there & then you read all the writings of St. John of the Cross & St. Theresa Avila & on & on, all the mystics & visionaries in recorded history & you say 'Well, they can't all be nuts, they must be talking about something.'" They can't all be nuts. Those words stayed with me, perhaps more than scripture.

He reminded us of the first of the Buddha's Four Noble Truths: we suffer. Anything that is stuck in time, Ram Dass wrote, is going to pass away and hence we suffer. And on the very same page he quoted Christian scripture: lay not up your treasures where moth and dust doth corrupt. On the same page. That was my first brush with what some call East-West, the dialogue between Christians and the Eastern religions.

I remember the Carolina mornings when I'd try to meditate before a candle flame, a book of instructions open on the floor beside me. The giving up such practice before it could take root. The glimmers of intellectual understanding. Mulling over eternity. Letting go. The distance I went to shed whatever was holding me back. Literal distance: long, arduous hiking trips into the backcountry where for days I forswore the comfort that ordinarily protected me from contemplating my own death, my puny temporality. Inner distance: the hallucinogens that freed me from time's yoke for a night. And here I am at a Catholic monastery about sixty miles from Union Hospital in Terre Haute, where I was born. I had to come all that way to find what I'd been looking for. So close to home.

V

Dr. Norbu is a tall, slender man in his seventies, slightly balding, smiling. Like many tall men he bends over a little to speak to you, a humble gesture. He wears glasses; his skin is rosy-brown. His jacket is pin-striped, his sweater vest maroon.

Dr. Thubten Jigme Norbu, retired Professor of Uralic and Altaic Studies at Indiana University, was born in Tibet in 1922. He entered the monastery at age eight and by the age of eighteen he was Abbot of Kumbum, leader of three thousand monks, one thousand households, thirty temples, and seventy hermitages. He left monastic life in 1951, came to the United States, and worked on behalf of Tibetans who were and are being persecuted by the Chinese. It is estimated that 1.2 million Tibetans have been tortured and killed.

To draw attention to the plight of the Tibetan people, 100,000 of whom are presently in exile in India, Dr. Norbu began his walks. In 1995 he walked from Bloomington to Indianapolis to raise consciousness about Tibet. In 1996 Dr. Norbu walked from Washington, D.C., to New York City and delivered a message to the secretary-general of the United Nations, regarding the Tibetan persecution. I am intensely curious about these walks – how it felt physically, what troubles he might have had along the way, what blessings, how strangers reacted.

In the chapel foyer I tuck a Breaking Bread songbook under my arm: I hope I have the chance to ask him about the walks.

The chapel is human-scale, with clear windows letting in a slant of afternoon autumn light. A wide Benedictine cross, hammered of metal and adorned with beech leaves, seems to nearly take flight at the right of the altar. Some senior sisters are dressed in black and white habits; some are dressed in Sunday best, dresses,

27

skirts; and some are casually dressed, in slacks or sweats, as though they've just come from a chore. One young sister, I can't help but notice, has two pierced earrings in one earlobe. We are mostly women, and our voices answer back and forth across the chapel, like the delicate voices of girls, psalm to psalm. When it is Dr. Norbu's turn to stand at the lectern, he offers a blessing for all sentient beings. We pray for people persecuted because of their religious practices. All people.

During the simple supper, the chicken soup, the bread and lemonade, I am seated beside Dr. Norbu. I ask him: How did your body react to the walk? Did you lose weight? No, no, he says, grinning, I stopped along the way and ate many french fries at McDonald's!

A Greek Orthodox couple are seated across from me. Strikingly beautiful, sensual, strong: she with big blond hair, heels and stockings, he with a wide handsome brow, smiling eyes, his white shirt crisp and glowing. They look as though they've just returned from Martinique. When Sister Meg gives Dr. Norbu the gift of an icon—the Blessed Mother and the Baby Jesus—the Greek Orthodox man leans forward, tells Dr. Norbu the legend of the first icon. It is said that Luke painted the first icon on a plank of wood taken from the table at the Last Supper. This story pleases everyone.

VI

Before he goes, Dr. Norbu demonstrates the three-point bow he practices before his own icons. The bow is a gesture I have an affinity for. It seems to be an interfaith gesture, signifying humility, gratitude, an acknowledgement of blessedness. "Blessedness," Nietzsche wrote, "is not promised, it is not tied to any conditions: it is the only reality." I first noticed the bow when I taught summer school at Choate two years ago. A gentle Thai boy would bow to me after I'd helped him untangle the snarl of nouns and verbs, prepositional phrases. I would bow back. Last summer at the Sacred Earth, Sacred Self Conference in Prescott, Arizona, Buddhist musicans and speakers would bow in response to applause. After that, I began to see the bow at Mass, a gesture I'd taken for granted, accepting it as priestly routine. What I like about bowing is this: it is a second's prayer, a flicker of intention to open to grace. Put your palms together heavenward, stop out of time, where joy resides.

VII

In the long hallway connecting one dining area to another in the monastery there are photographs of the Dalai Lama, talking, teaching, in his burnt-orange and yellow robes, one shoulder bare, that look of pure clear attention on his face.

On a stair landing across from a statue of the sweet-tempered Blessed Mother are nine cotton banners, embroidered with the words of wise women:

Adrienne Rich: I have been trying to give birth to myself.
Teresa of Avila: There is no better crucible for testing prayer than compassion.
Joan Chillister: If you seek God, seek from within yourself.
Susan Griffin: Oh, this knowledge of what we are is becoming clear.
Hildegard of Bingen: Holy persons draw to themselves all that is earthly.
Julian of Norwich: The fullness of joy is to behold God in everything.
Mechtild of Magdeburg: How should one live? Live welcoming all.

Simone Weil: One should identify with the universe itself.
Starhawk: We can know the dark and dream it into a new image.

In the library I took note of the long row of Merton's books. One of them has an introduction by Thich Nhat Hanh, the Buddhist monk from Vietnam.

I am of two minds: happy to know that this dialogue has a solidity about it; it is a path already hacked out of the wilderness by those who've gone before; and I'm regretful that I did not discover it before. But all that—the happiness, the regret—could become clinging. And the Diamond Sutra instructs us to have minds that cling to nothing.

The Dalai Lama has written: "A place initially becomes holy by the power of the individual spiritual practitioner who lives there. The power of an individual's spiritual realizations in some sense 'charges' the place. The place in turn can 'charge' the individuals who visit there." In Beech Grove it's dark outside; winter will be here soon. The long gray Indiana winter. But Our Lady of Grace Monastery is a charged spiritual place, and within the many winters the Beech Grove Benedictines have weathered, they've found the fire inside, what John of the Cross, the sixteenth-century Christian mystic, called the lucky dark, a place where all that is earthly is drawn. And welcomed.

KADDISH

Bert Stern

I spend a lot of time with the dead. Or I tell myself this for comfort. I want the dead to be companionable. I'm an old man, near the border between my realm and theirs. I want a little society between us. Old friends come, we sit down, we talk a little. When I write a poem that pleases me I think of Doc Kemp, wonder if he's drinking in heaven and if I'm writing well enough for his tough Yankee standards. I want to give him a present across the boundary. I think of the Greek steles, how the woman reaches for the jewel box her maid offers her, how the husband reaches toward the wife. In these there is always a breach, a space between the hands that wish to touch, between the woman's fingers and the jewel box. But still, we reach to touch.

When my colleague Owen Duston died, I prayed in my heart that he would somehow pass on his great learning to me so that it not be lost forever. I grieved terribly for his mind and imagination when I realized that this would not happen–as I did for his voice and smile, and his passion for teaching.

John Swan's laughter wraps around me often, like his beautiful old tallis that his wife Susan gave me after he died. John is the most hilarious, the most Rabelaisian of my dead, so I'm very glad to have him. But if he's my most amiable ghost, he's also the fiercest. An absolutist for the First Amendment, he worked in his writing toward "a way to allow the maximum breathing room for a multiplicity of sometimes hostile beliefs which must now share, in an increasingly literal sense, the same space." And he loved music with the same passion. He could hardly breathe anymore by the time he died, hadn't been able for a long time, except with the machine he hated. But to the end he never stopped thinking and writing and listening to music,

the violin he couldn't play any longer sitting next to the chair he could no longer rise from.

My father whom I could hardly talk to in life is closer to me now. We understood each other for a moment when he was dying of a stroke and couldn't speak. He was embarrassed. He hated people to see him naked and now the nurses had to help him shit. It was terrible for him. And he couldn't talk. What's left of a man when he can't speak? But I tried to meet him in this place he was locked in, and I loved him there, maybe for the first time. He had no choice but to allow my tenderness, I had no choice but to give it. This was new to us and we still have it, so we can meet at last in good and loving company.

With my mother things have gone less well. She was bitter over her death. Why not? She was forty-four, and life had tricked her out of everything. She'd invested a lot of hopes in me, but I wasn't any good to her at the time. I was busy becoming an intellectual, and it was my understanding at that time that intellectuals did not love their mothers. So I'm still trying to make peace with her, forty years after she died.

What does it mean for my own death, these visitations, these companionships, these ongoing quarrels? Maybe I just want to think that the conversation keeps going. Though in the end the dead must have better business than to keep company with the living, we can't know very much about that business. Not in advance. Homer thought that the dead longed eternally for the things we have every day–the simple sun, life in the body. Others have thought they must be greatly relieved to throw all that off. I only know that for me, as for Wallace Stevens, death is the mother of much beauty and poignancy.

So it seemed natural for me to come to the Jewish cemetery in Indianapolis. And not just to keep company with the dead. I'm trying to get back in touch with my Jewishness. I've gone back to *shul* (synagogue) a couple of times in the last few years, and I've liked it. I'm no longer bored there as I was when I was a kid. And I'm an old man. So I went and made my visit.

The first time wasn't so good. I rode around south Indianapolis for a long time looking for the cemetery. I knew it was on South Meridian and I thought the search would be easy. But though I found all kinds of cemeteries, they weren't Jewish. Sometimes I could tell at once because the figure of Our Lady was on the gate, sometimes I could tell by crosses. A few times I had to go inside and read the names.

I was on a motorcycle and this made things awkward. Once I asked a lady who was putting flowers on a grave if she knew where the Jewish cemetery was. Asking her was stupid, but I'd already come in on the bike, and I wanted her to know I wasn't a raw interloper, in my leather jacket. Another time I asked two boys in black, sitting on the steps of a funeral parlor, with a ceremony going on inside. They didn't know either, and I felt that Jewish matters were at best very remote from them.

I asked realtors and gas station attendants. Nobody could tell me, though the realtor was very nice, and looked in the phone book for me, and suggested I check at the funeral parlor—the one I'd already been to, where the boys couldn't tell me.

I was embarrassed to give up my search. I'd left the house in a hurry, hardly hearing my wife's question, "Do you know where it is?" But give it up I did, to ride back the fifty miles in mid-August heat, disheartened. The quest was starting under bad auspices.

But the project was important to me. Although I'm not a good Jew, I'm trying to get better, and burial is important to Jews. Reform Judaism has softened or abandoned some of the traditional strictures, and it is true, as J. F. Moore says in his classic work on Rabbinic Judaism, that "Any attempt to systematize the Jewish notions of the hereafter imposes upon them an order and consistency which does not exist in them." Still, notions prevail. If a Jew says that he doesn't want to be buried, Jewish law insists that we must not listen to him. The dead must submit to the earth. They need to be born again out of its womb. They need to be transformed by the forces of fire and water and air, and earth itself. They need to rot and be broken down into their parts, so as to return to their source and there renew themselves into the next realm. Traditionally, the coffin is of cheap pine, without nails. "From dust thou art and to dust thou shalt return."

This must be a process of rot, not fire. The only exception to be made is for the victims of the Holocaust, to whom special care is given, so that they can be placed before God as little children are placed in the arms of a loving father.

Some Jews—probably not many—think that, in cases other than those of the martyrs, cremation or improper burial brings unspeakable consequences. I read from a text on Jewish burial put out by Shamash ("a Jewish Internet Consortium"):

> If a Jew does not receive proper burial, his soul will literally roll around in the world of imaginations. Unable to find its resting place, the soul is thrown between the sphere of this world and the heavenly world. This causes devils with 10, 6, or 3 faces to take control of the lost soul. They kick it or throw it around. They may squeeze it into a tiny stone or cut it into minute pieces. They might change it into a donkey, snake, monkey or cat.

An improperly buried body "will be whipped by devils and will feel pain as if it were still alive." The body will further "be bombarded by ice balls which are colder than any temperature in our earthly experience. We can imagine 1000 degrees F below zero! The body will feel the continuous pain of being frozen to death but the relief of death will never come to stop the pain."

Do I believe this? No, but it makes me uneasy. At one time my wife and I had talked about cremation. Now I tell her I'd prefer to be buried in a plain pine box in a Jewish cemetery.

In the meantime, still kicking, I got a better idea where the cemetery is and learned the name of the head of the Jewish Historical Society in Indianapolis. And before I visited the cemetery and interviewed the historian, I went to see a friend, a psychoanalyst, with whom I talked about spiritual matters. I told him about the project, and asked if he'd ever been to the cemetery. I could see that he was caught short by my question. It turned out that his father was buried there and he hadn't been back since the funeral. So we arranged to go together.

Leo Rosten tells the story of a legendary *zeyde* (grandfather) known as "the Saint of Shpolle." Heartsick over the sufferings of the Jews and the injustices of the world he decided to put God on trial. So he gathered nine friends to serve as judges, himself being the tenth needed for a *minyan*, and summoned the Almighty to appear on the witness stand. (Since God is everywhere, the *zeyde* simply closed the door.)

For three days and nights the remarkable court stayed in session. They presented charges, devised defenses, pondered, prayed, fasted, consulted the Torah and the Talmud. And in the end, in solemn consensus, they issued their verdict: God was guilty—on two counts: first, He had created the spirit of Evil and then let it loose among innocent and pliable people; and second, He clearly failed to provide poor widows and orphans with decent food and shelter.

But the *zeyde's* court did not find God guilty on account of death. Indeed, one Talmudist, glossing the text: "And God saw all that He had made, and behold it was very good," observed: 'Behold it was very good'—this refers to death." (The reasoning here, Rabbis Sandy and Dennis Sasso inform me, depends on Hebrew word play: *tov m'od* ("Behold it was very good") sounds like *tov mot* ("good death," meaning death is good).

Still, Jews find no easy comfort for death. The Babylonian Talmud tells how Rabbi Nahman begged a disciple to tell the angel of death not to torture him. When the disciple replied, "You're a man of great honor, you may speak directly to him," Nahman answered: "Who is honored, who is distinguished, who is singled out before the angel of death?"

But when, after his death, Nahman showed himself to this same disciple, and the disciple asked: "Did you suffer much pain?" Nahman replied; "It was easy as taking a hair from a pitcher of milk. But were God to say to me, 'Go back to the world as you were before,' I would not want to go. For the fear of death is so great there."

Moses himself is said to have wrestled with all his dying strength against the angel of death until a heavenly voice declared: "Enough, Moses, the time of your death has come." And even then, though Moses obeyed the command and lay down and closed his eyes and folded his hands across his chest, his soul, in a final act of rebellion, refused to leave his body. Peace came at last, according to the legend, only when "God kissed Moses and took away his soul with a kiss of the mouth. And God wept."

But maybe the most affecting Jewish story about death concerns Rabbi Eleazar ben Pedat, who had suffered the death of ten sons in their youth, and who was so poor at the time of his death that he lived in a room without a window. He was visited at his deathbed by Rabbi Johanan ben Nappaha, a man so beautiful that light shone from his body.

Finding Eleazar in darkness, Johanan bared his arm so that light radiated from it, and Eleazar began to cry. Johanan tried to comfort

32

him. Was he weeping because he had not studied enough? Because of his poverty? Because none of his children would survive him? For each of these griefs Johanan offered comfort.

But in the end Eleazar replied, "I'm weeping because of your beauty, which will wither in the earth."

Johanan said to him: "You are right to cry over that."

And they both wept.

These stories gathered around the cemetery visit. What I take from them is a kind of embrace between *Gevurah*, God's implacable law, and *Chesed*, his mercy. We are right to cry. We wrestle with the Angel of Death because the fear of death is very great here. Yet we need to be able to say, with Rabbi Meir, "'Behold it was very good'—this refers to death."

I prepared myself with history as well as stories. There were three Jews in Indianapolis in 1849: Alexander and Sarah Franco, and Moses Woolf. By 1856 the Indianapolis Hebrew Congregation was established by the forty-five men who approved the constitution and by-laws. At the congregation's organizational meeting, $125 was pledged for purchase of cemetery land. I learned all this from Tevie Jacobs, the eighty-eight-year-old President of the Jewish Historical Society. It's traditional, Jacobs told me, for the cemetery to come first, even before the synagogue, so important it is for a Jew to be buried in hallowed ground.

The money these pioneers collected to buy land for a cemetery wasn't much, and they were obliged to buy cheap—a parcel at the southern edge of town, off Meridian on Kelly Street. Today the Jewish Cemetery that began nearly one hundred and forty years ago is nearly full, so a new one has begun. Back then, as now, it was an area of dumps, low land, a place for fever, that nobody who could choose better wanted. The Catholics landed here too, presumably for the same reasons, and their cemetery is shoulder-to-shoulder to the Jewish one,

across Kelly Street. Later, when I told Max Nelson, owner of Meridian Hills Mortuary, about the difficulty I'd had finding the Jewish Cemetery, he nodded: the Christian cemeteries, most of them, anyway, were built on hills, with trees, with big entranceways on Meridian. But when the Hebrew Congregation bought their land, they didn't have much money. They were obliged to buy where the dumps were.

When the immigration of east European Jews began to accelerate after 1881, because Tzar Nicholas had begun to make anti-Semitism part of his antirevolutionary policy, new waves reached Indianapolis, and fresh congregations—Polish, Russian, Hungarian—were formed. The new immigrants came with old world beliefs and customs, they spoke Yiddish, and their religious practice was, as L.C. Rudolph puts it in *Hoosier Faiths*, "loud and long." None of this was congenial to the earlier, Americanized German population that worshipped in the Reform Hebrew Congregation.

The situation in Indianapolis could not have been very different from what Abraham Cronbach discovered when he arrived in South Bend in 1906 to be rabbi at the "ultra-liberal" Temple Beth-El. As Rudolph reports, the ultra-liberal congregation wanted services only on the "High Holidays," they wanted less preaching on the Torah, more discussions of "questions of the day," and they wanted no Hebrew classes. Indeed, as Cronbach soon discovered, this temple had been organized "to demonstrate to the Gentiles that all Jews were not as indecorous as the 'Pollacks'—Jews of east European origin." Some members of the new congregation, before they *were* a congregation, had attended the funeral of an acquaintance who had kept some of the old ways. They were so "shocked at the bedlam of the Orthodox obsequies" that they organized a synagogue more or less at once, "for the purpose of convincing the Gentiles that there are Jews among whom funerals can be solemn and dignified."

So the new east European immigrants necessarily started their own synagogues and benevolent societies. And, of course, their own cemeteries. There was the Polish *Sharah Tefilla* (Gates of Prayer), the Russian *Knesses Israel* (Assembly of Israel–or of Jewish people), and the Hungarian *Ohev Zedeck*, which in 1928 merged with *Beth-El* synagogue to become *Beth-El Zedeck*, still a thriving congregation. The poorest of the synagogues, *Ezras Achim* was known as the "peddler's congregation" because so many peddlers belonged to it. And they too had a cemetery, right there, in south Indianapolis, where in life they eked out a living by picking up metal scrap no one else wanted and finding a market for it. But while all these synagogues were autonomous, and all of them something of an embarrassment to the older Jewish residents, in death a kind of democracy necessarily prevailed. The new cemeteries were all situated on the same acres that the Hebrew Congregation had purchased, each set off from the others primarily by its individual gate. And although the Reform funeral services would have been gentrified, and largely in English, while the others had the look and sound of the peasant heritages they'd derived from, the funeral processions bore a common stamp: the funeral took place at home, and the body was carried in a rough cart to the cemetery, while the mourners, old and young, lame and able, walked behind.

Until recent times, the Jewish population of Indianapolis stayed in the section where it began. (As late as the 1950s, according to Max Nelson, one of the partners in Meridian Hills Mortuary, 70 percent of the city's ten thousand Jews still lived "within a stone throw of Shapiro's Delicatessen.") The new cemeteries, adjacent to the old one, spread west toward Bluff Street. Some of the congregations associated with them died out, but the cemeteries remain as a kind of geological record of Indianapolis's Jewish community.

In the passion of my research, I'd lost my place in my story. I am a Jew who has attended only two Jewish funerals, my mother's and my father's, and I remember neither of them. Of my mother's funeral I remember only the family sitting around at the table afterwards, eating and drinking, telling stories, laughing. I was outraged and bewildered. Whatever the funeral ceremony had done for them it had done nothing for me. In my pain and confusion I felt myself utterly alone. And I'd never even observed the anniversaries of my parents' deaths. But now as I immersed myself in Jewish burial rite, the meaning and use of these rituals disclosed themselves to me. Precisely to these moments when the mourner feels most alone ritual brings solace by weaving personal loss back into the fabric of the universal. And I found myself drawn to the austere order of Jewish funeral practice.

Jewish burial customs are simple, but highly charged. All ostentation is banned–no flowers or music. The body must be ritually washed and purified by members of the *Chevra Kaddishah*, "The Sacred Society," anonymous, a bit ghostly, who perform these duties as a service to the community and as a *mitzvah*, an act of piety that promises eternal rewards. While awaiting burial, the body must not be left unattended, but watched over by a pious Jewish person, who recites psalms, and by the members of *Chrevra Kaddishah*.

The body is not to be embalmed, not to be viewed in the casket, and must be buried, not incinerated. The body is to be wrapped in a white shroud, symbolizing the equality of all before the Almighty. The mourners are expected to tear their garments, as King David did when he learned of the death of his son Absalom. Sometimes, this tearing, known as *K'ria*, is done symbolically, by the pinning on of a torn black ribbon. And, finally, the grave is to be filled until a mound is formed. Participation in the filling of the grave is a religious privilege and duty. Sometimes members of the family throw in the first handfuls, as a gesture of acquiescence.

I asked Tevie Jacobs whether people still hold to the belief that those not properly buried are exposed to demons. He answered with wonderful Jewish obliquity: "Well, Jews all try to be buried in a Jewish cemetery." Jews whose families can't afford to buy a plot are buried nonetheless in a Jewish cemetery, thanks to the generosity of congregations and the Jewish Federation of Greater Indianapolis. And though the Jewish cemeteries are congregational, a Jew who isn't a member of a congregation can still be buried in a congregational cemetery.

Remembrance of the dead is elaborately ritualized. This interested me especially, because the process of remembering the dead has been crucial for me in my own search for self-identity. For a long time I had lived as if I were self-created. And it was only when I began to understand how deeply I was the fulfillment of other people's dreams that I began to know who I was. Now I began to glimpse in the details of the ritual a means of making overt the cycles of pain and healing, severence and reunion, that mark our relations with our dead.

For seven days the mourners "sit *shiva*," a seven-day period of grieving in which men don't wash and men and women both neglect their personal appearance. Friends provide them with food during this period. The mourners are given utterly to their grief. They sit uncomfortably on benches or on the floor.

This is followed by a twenty-three-day period called *sheloshim*, during which the bereaved persons are weaned from their grief and gradually come back to their normal lives. But mourners continue to say *kaddish*, the prayer for the dead, every morning and evening for eleven months, and after that, once a year, on the anniversary of the death.

And the dead are remembered by the community as well. On the Day of Atonement, Yom Kippur, as on Passover, Shavuot, and Sukkot, each denomination has religious services at the cemeteries. And every service in the synagogue ends with the recital of the *kaddish*.

In all this I discover that my own interest in the dead, like other character traits I used to think of as personal idiosyncracies, comes to me by way of the culture I was raised in, and from which I learned that history looks both ways. When I visited Max Nelson, a Jewish funeral director, he emphasized with deep feeling the importance of remembering. We, the living, need the assurance that ritualized memory gives us. The living owe this debt to the dead, and in paying it, they give something to themselves as well—the anticipatory gift that they too may be remembered.

In his youth, when Mr. Nelson was politically active, Senator Wayne Morris was a great hero of his. Now who remembers him, he wonders, when did you last hear his name? We owe these remembrances to one another. "My mother's not going to know I put a little rock on her grave. But people drive by and they think, he hasn't forgotten."

I had arrived a little early at the Meridian Hills Mortuary where I was to meet Mr. Nelson. There, on the 1300 block of West 86th, in the midst of strip malls and unabated shlock of every commercial order, I sat in the parking lot, gathering my thoughts; they weren't pretty thoughts. I remembered *The Loved One* and *The American Way of Death*. I thought, how can one who makes condolence one's business not be vulgar and false? How can one who beautifies the irretrievable not be macabre?

But even as these thoughts came to my mind I knew they belonged to a younger and angrier man. I've known precious acts of kindness at the hands of undertakers. And oddly, not long ago, I believe that I helped create a funeral director. A student of mine had become enchanted with James Agee's articulate silence and had written a sweet and attentive essay on the subject. When I saw him after a long interval he told me that he'd discovered what to do with his life—he was going to undertakers' school, thus to become, presumably, a kind of groom of silence.

When I entered the Meridian Hills Mortuary it was a familiar and disturbing scene. I walked down a corridor with large assembly rooms on each side. Everywhere the carpets were thick, and the hushing of my own feet was a little uncanny. The silence said louder than words that this place was about absence, not presence. I don't know if I'd expected a receptionist, but there was no one in sight. When I heard voices I steered toward them with a feeling of relief. A man and a woman were talking in an office. She looked up, I told her who I was, and the man introduced himself as Max Nelson and invited me into his inner office.

I liked Mr. Nelson at once, and thought that he was just the kind of person I would wish to be buried by. He's big and good-looking, full of life, and, by force of the mysterious code I still hardly understand, unmistakably Jewish. Maybe I mean no more than a kind of worldly kindness, a skeptical piety, a peculiar balance between the concerns of this world and of the next. Mr. Nelson did not pretend to be fundamentalist in his piety. Once, explaining delicately that, in the case of a terrible accident in which some limb is severed, the limb is to be placed in the coffin against the prospect of the end of time, when everyone will be resurrected, he remarked: "If you believe that you believe anything."

I asked him about the threats of torture by demons that I'd read about, and he shook his head, skeptical and amused. He'd never heard of this. Judaism is a positive religion, he said. The *mitzvoh* (the commandments and the acts we perform to keep them) encourage people to live good and clean lives. Nobody's threatened by hell fire and brimstone if they don't practice the 613 *mitzvoh*. As to burial, there are important *mitzvoh* regarding the bathing and dressing and burying of the dead. These are good practices for the living to do, kinds of courtesy to the dead. Maybe some misguided individuals think of such *mitzvoh* as threats. Regrettably, Mr. Nelson added, there's plenty of *mishigas* (craziness) in Judaism as there is everywhere else.

Yet when it came to the practice of the burial mitvoth, these he described lovingly. Yes, a man is wrapped in his *tallis* (prayer shawl) when he is buried, one piece of the fringe cut off to symbolize that he is no longer able to practice God's laws. Mr. Nelson took a kind of epic pride in his record for carrying out burials expeditiously, as tradition dictates. A burial will be delayed as necessary to allow mourners to travel from far places, he explained, but almost never for weather. "When a Jew is going to be buried, we defy all elements. I've only delayed a funeral once because of weather."

In the end I come to the cemetery alone. The friend who was going to accompany me, a man five years older than myself, has been sick all year, and now he's sick again. I worry about him as I finally park on Kelly Street. The cemetery is in a poor part of town, a mishmash of dejected houses and humiliated convenience stores and taverns, truck parks, abrasive industry. There's a big fire just out of sight nearby. I hear sirens, and a towering cloud of churning smoke hovers not far from the cemetery itself.

It's just noon as I walk through the eastern gate, on a hot day, threats of thunderstorms in the clouds. Almost as soon as I set foot inside I come to a stone with a picture of a young girl on it: she was Rachel Hope Valentine, and she died six years ago, at the age of fifteen. "Walk softly," the stone pleads, "for a beautiful dream lies buried here."

That's what the cemetery was from the first, a place of buried dreams. In October 1860, when there couldn't have been many more people in the nebulous Hebrew Congregation than the original fourteen members who had founded it in 1856, the warden of the cemetery presented a report on "the Number of More Deceased" since he took office the previous December. All but two of those dead were children, several of them infants, like the "Child buried of Myer Myer, which had no name yet."

But over the years the democracy of death takes in all ages. After all, one of the Hebrew names for cemetery is *Beit Olam*, community of the whole. Cohens are here, and Lowensteins, and Grundigs, Salingers, Kaminskys, Kaufmans. Many of the stones are carved with Jewish stars, some with Menorahs. Here and there, leaves and flowers, or the Masonic symbols. On one stone an open book is chiseled over the name "Weill," the wife's name on the left, the husband's on the right. They died in the same year.

There are few trees here, and the stones are pressed closely together. There are few paths, either, and to look closely at an individual stone, I often have to tread precariously close to a neighboring grave site. "So many, I had not thought death had undone so many," Dante lamented in Hell, and I lament here with him. But deeper than the lament another knowledge rises: the world belongs to the dead more than to the living. And across the street, literally within a stone's throw, lest one doubt the wide scope of death's dominion, the Catholic cemetery is spread out, leading me to wonder how firmly our demarcations survive the chemistry that goes on under the ground.

The Gundelfins are laid out in a wide row of small stones that stand before the commanding stone that bears the family name. One of the stones bears the name of a son who died in 1888, many years before his father.

I find a stone that goes back to 1876, nearly indecipherable, though a lamb carved on it still lies in sharp relief. On the stone next to it only a few scattered letters are discernible, and some quiet utterances of mold.

"Beloved husband, beloved wife." "Forever in our hearts." "Abraham Jacob, Fanny Goodman, Loving Parents." So much utterance, nearly mute, those who uttered their grief, many of them, themselves under the ground, the rest of us waiting in turn. How quickly the dead become companionable, and the *Beit Olam* opens its doors to us. A cemetery, after all, is also called

Beit Hahayyim, the house of the living, lest we miss the point. But for the heart it is the gate of remembrance, and of continuity. Moses received the Torah at Sinai and handed it down to Joshua; Joshua, to the elders; the elders, to the prophets. And so it is handed down today, as children receive it in their arms as they become *B'nai Mitzvah*, in a transmission that flows from the dead to the living, from God to humankind.

"Just art Thou, O Lord, in causing death and life; thou in whose hand all living beings are kept, far be it from thee to blot out remembrance; let Thy eyes be open to us in mercy; for Thine, O Lord, is mercy and forgiveness." So the Jewish funeral service asserts, and I say, Amen to that. Remembrance is what the living give to the dead; the rest, as far as we are concerned, is silence, yet we speak the words: *loving father, loving wife, here lies a beautiful dream,* over gravestones open to the sun.

Then, suddenly, it starts to rain, on the living and the dead. The sky is churning now, with the face of one who doesn't make fine distinctions. The last gravestone I really look at before running for the car back on Kelly Street marks the graves of Abe and Fannie Epstein. Somebody has put three small stones on the marker.

In the old days, orthodox rogues who called themselves "Reb" this or "Reb" that hung around the cemetery waiting for grievers, and for a few dollars would say prayers for the departed. Despite the rain, I'd willingly pay now for the service. My visit wants a ritual close. These dead have become my dead. But the only human figure in sight isn't a bearded man in black hat and caftan, with *payess* (hairlocks) hanging over his ears, but a boy without a shirt. He's been cutting grass just outside the gate, and now he's running helter-skelter through it, into the cemetery and the groundskeeper's shack, for shelter.

Mallah A. Mordoh

I am Jewish. Fifty years ago, to speak those three simple words would mean death to 6 million of my fellow Jews. At this, the 50 year anniversary of the Holocaust, I have given much thought and reflection as to what being Jewish means to me.

My family's history is one of persecution also, albeit, a persecution different than the horror of the Holocaust. You see, my heritage is that of a Sephardic Jew. The Sephardim originated in Spain. In 1492, the Sephardic Jews were expelled from Spain due to religious persecution. My ancestors settled in Solonika, a city located in between Greece and Turkey. Greece and Turkey were in constant battle as to the ownership of Solonika. There was one thing that they could agree upon, however, that neither country desired a Jewish population. Because of the constant prejudices against our people, my grandparents immigrated to the United States in the early 1900's arriving in Indianapolis in 1913.

own social clubs. My grandfather, Mallah Mordoh, was one of the original founders of the Etz Chaim synagogue which is still thriving today. Finally, after many years had passed, the Sephardim were accepted by the Ashkenazim as part of the Jewish community as a whole.

In many ways, the prejudice that my grandparents experienced upon their arrival in Indianapolis, has made me that much stronger in my religious beliefs. The strength that my grandfather and his peers showed in not allowing the ways of the Sephardim to die have made my dedication to continuance of the Etz Chaim a driving force in my life. I feel proud to be a Sephardic Jew. It is a tradition that I am passing along to my son, Alan. Although Alan is the product of an "intermarriage" (my wife is of Ashkenazic heritage), he is learning the traditions of both sects of Judaism. I am passing along to him what my grandparents and parents have passed on to me, that being Jewish is to be born into a history rich in tradition and filled with courage.

Because of their Spanish heritage and inability to speak Yiddish, the Sephardim in Indianapolis were not thought of as "real" Jews by the Ashkenazim. The Sephardim were forced to form their own synagogue, perform their own burials, and form their

I am Jewish. Due to the strength and courage of my forebears, I can say those words proudly and freely in 1997 America. I will do my best to assure that 50 years from now, my son will also be able to do likewise.

38

Sharon Mishkin

I grew up in Brooklyn, New York, during and just after World War II. It was a most glorious time and place to be Jewish. Everyone I knew was Jewish and life was sweet and safe.

It wasn't until many years later that I realized that the people I grew up with were Jews who did not practice their religion. My own parents were completely nonobservant; they did however send my brother and me to Hebrew School.

Educational and marital choices found me in Indiana in

the 1960s. It was only with the birth of our three children that religious affiliation became important to me. Living in a city with a small Jewish population was also a force in pointing me toward affiliation and shaping a Jewish identity. Returning to Hebrew School introduced me to women who would influence my life forever. I had now met people who lived their lives Jewishly. I decided that I would try to follow their examples. The awakening of Jewish feminism in the last two decades also forced me to evaluate and reevaluate my place in Judaism and to try to find a "comfort zone" in my everyday practice.

Living Jewishly in America now means education and choice. We can avail ourselves of the many forms of Jewish education available to us now. We are able to choose that branch of Judaism which makes sense to us intellectually and emotionally; in my case that choice happens to be Reconstructionism.

As American Jews, we can live in a Jewishly pluralistic society, not always agreeing on our practices, but knowing that we are cousins in a beautiful extended family.

We are now more than fifty years post-holocaust and I feel optimistic about Judaism in America. We have and always will have Jews leaving our faith, whether by indifference or choice. We are without the outside hate forces which kept so many of us Jewish over the millennia. We now have people choosing to be Jewish, whether they were born Jewish or seeking a new spiritual identity. Hopefully, our open society will permit all seekers to find their Jewish place.

39

Joshua Zerin

Living in a democratic and free society 50 years after the Holocaust, I and my family enjoy being able to openly practice our religion. In years past and in other places, Jews have had to hide their practice of Judaism. I am happy to say that I have not seen or experienced very much, if any, anti-Semitism in my own life, particularly at school, or in my life generally. Unfortunately, I and my family know that there is still anti-Semitism in the world. In our own lives, we try to prevent anti-Semitism by setting an example through being good people and good Jews. I teach my friends about Judaism and my mother goes to our schools to talk about Jewish traditions on holidays like Chanuka and Passover. My brothers and my sisters also teach their friends about Judaism. When we miss school days on Jewish holidays so that we can go to synagogue, I do not feel uncomfortable, because I realize that, in America, I am free to be Jewish.

Being Jewish is a source of personal pride to me. I enjoy the privileges and responsibilities of being a Jew, and I am sure that many other (unfortunately not all) Jews around the world feel the same way. Attending religious school, being a teacher's aide there and participating in my temple's youth group are just a few of the many responsibilities I must face as I grow up in my community. With the skills I learn at home and in religious and Hebrew schools, I am able to participate in services and observe holidays. Being able to attend a Jewish camp is also a privilege I enjoy. I am able to celebrate holidays there and see how different Jews pray and observe Judaism.

Through education people learn to be tolerant of others. It is my hope that for all time people will continue to learn to accept each other and respect one another.

Pavl Waisburd

Almost all my life I spent in the former Soviet Union, where to be a Jew meant to be a person who was constantly subjected to discrimination because of his Jewish origin. In the former Soviet Union the synagogues were closed, the Jewish educational institutions didn't exist at all, and the Jews were deprived of their national originality. Jewish education and activities were persecuted and severely punished.

In 1990 our family immigrated to the USA and came to Indianapolis. Return to our Jewish national roots, acquaintance with the basis of Judaism became one of our most important goals here in the USA. All my grandchildren started their school in Hebrew Academy of Indianapolis, which two of them graduated this year and the youngest is still attending, getting a very solid Jewish education. The whole family joined the congregation Bel-El Zedeck. Step by step we learn Judaism by reading the Torah and literature on the religious problem and history of Jewish people, a history of keeping their religion and originality despite persecution and oppression. In the twentieth century the Jewish people under-

went one of the most terrible tragedies in their history: Holocaust. At the same time we witnessed the great miracle— the state of Israel rebuilt.

Summarizing, to me to be Jewish at the edge of the millennium in Indianapolis and anywhere means:

1. To give a young generation Jewish education

2. To keep Jewish traditions

3. To be active in social and political movements, oriented on solving social and racial problems in this country and in the world. Growth of that kind of problems always leads to the growth of anti-Semitism.

4. To support in all possible ways economic development of Israel and her fight for security.

I'm sure, that on this path the Jews will be able to preserve the principles of Judaism, for which their ancestors endured incredible persecutions during the four thousand years of their history.

41

STILL CATHOLIC
Dan Carpenter

I had no need
for a mentor, nor for you to be one;
but I was once more
your chosen sister, and you
my chosen brother.
We heard strong harmonies begin to fill
the arching stone,
sounds that had risen here through centuries.
      — Denise Levertov, from "To R. D., March 4, 1988"

was maybe five, six years old, barely at the beginnings of memory, and I thought I was going to die. I, my family, all the hundreds of people under the shadowed ceiling and yellow stained-glass chandeliers of St. Patrick's Church. It felt wrong in the first place, being there on a week night; and the sight of those swords, hoisted over the archbishop's head as he entered, convinced me the worst was at hand and the nonchalance of the adults was some sort of unspeakable trick. I turned to my mother in bewilderment that she did not have the look of one about to be slaughtered with her children. I did not understand these strangers with their Dracula costumes, their rasping blades. I didn't know what the sacrament of confirmation meant, nor what the pealing *Tantum ergo* and *Agnus Dei qui tollis peccata mundi* meant, nor whom the life-size plaster statues represented; but I knew what knives were for and I was as terrified as I could be without taking off running.

I already sensed that you didn't just up and leave church; not before Father had locked the golden chalice with the Blessed Sacrament behind its miniature golden sliding doors and had swooped with his retinue of gowned altar boys through the exit to the left of the monumental marble altar. You could faint in church, toppling over in a head-cracking clatter that thrilled your schoolmates because it looked like dying; you could die in church, of course; but you couldn't just walk out while mass was on, not even to escape executioners. Saints had died smiling, standing fast for faith under indescribable torture. If you had to pee, you offered it up. In college in the late 1960s, I could still feel a mild shock when a fellow who was in ROTC told me he'd walked out of mass in protest during an antiwar sermon. Mass was not up to you, any more than was the instrumentality of your death.

The black capes and plumed hats and sabers aren't displayed around Catholic churches so much any more. I haven't seen them in years except at an archbishop's funeral, and never have I seen them at my church, St. Thomas Aquinas. That's not to say they haven't been there, the white-gloved, gray-haired chosen men standing sentry over some ceremony; but if they've been there, they've been out of place and out of time. We tend to call on the Knights of Columbus these days for scholarships and fish fries, not martial readiness. At St. Thomas in particular, uniforms and weapons remind us of the soldiers and gangsters who used to terrorize our sister parish in Haiti, before the rebel priest Father Aristide and his revolution.

Ayiti—poor and black, free at last, with our help, and no thanks to the Vatican. Listen for such liberal scandal in our unique pocket of the Northside of Indianapolis, where we're multiracial, college-educated, widely traveled, warmed by still-fresh memories of open housing demonstrations and peace vigils. If you're divorced or gay and still don't want to leave a religion that condemns your behavior, St. Thomas is there. But we're not unanimous. We have dissent. Some of it—mutterings of "commie" and "fry 'em" and the nonsectarian "Jesus Christ"—even rears up to break the spell of our Sunday gatherings. Some of it comes from Catholics who want church the way they remember church.

We did not have antiwar and open-housing sermons at St. Pat's, but we had sermons about the Third Reich, only a few years out of the headlines, and about communism, its Godless successor. We heard from the pulpit the tale of one of their soldiers, taking a baby from its mother's arms as if to cuddle it and then dashing it like a chicken against the pavement. We were only a generation or two away from that nightmare Europe, many of us in the big family of big congregations on the near-Southside.

Fountain Square and St. Pat's were Irish Catholic, though not in the permeated and fortified way of a Boston immigrant church, or a New York or Chicago one. My grandmother believed in leprechauns along with the Transfiguration and the Immaculate Conception, but men of my father's generation drank their bottles of Wiedemann's and Oertel's 92 without songs or stories of the old country and without denunciations of kings. During the Depression, it is said, the Irish women would stand outside taverns on Shelby Street begging for some of the pittance their husbands were squandering inside; but even such stories, founded or not, had ceased to contribute to the "Irishness" of the neighborhood I knew.

Fountain Square also was Protestant in various manifestations, including Foursquare Gospel Tabernacle, where the whole building, and not just the choir loft, poured forth song, and not in Latin. Like movie cowboys spying from the trees on the Indian war council, we crept near their windows on Sunday nights to listen; and we used the Kentucky Bible Belters as foils for snobbery, until we lived elsewhere and discovered we all sounded pretty much the same—"yew" being every bit the social betrayer "y'all" was to a New Yorker or a Chicagoan.

St. Pat's was Irish Catholic and German Catholic and Italian Catholic in varying proportions at various times. Historically, in fact, the heavier Irish concentration was farther east, around St. Philip Neri and Holy Cross; German was Sacred Heart to the south; Italian was Holy Rosary hard by downtown on the north, the produce district.

The Italians were in business for themselves, and rich, we figured. A Thunderbird parked on the Southside surely would be one of theirs. Though we lived within blocks of them in that time before the great middle-class diaspora, we children met them in large numbers in the late 1950s, a couple years before my graduation, when St. Patrick School absorbed the students from Holy Rosary and the downtown school St. John's, where congregations and enrollments had shrunk with the early waves of exodus from the central city. The Irish and the Italians were about the most Catholic people in the world, but the Donahues and McGreevys and the English-surnamed Carpenters anticipated the arrival of the Caitos and Murellos and Spicuzzas with as much unease as people in suburban schools would feel toward black kids bused out from the inner city in the early 1980s. "One thing you'll notice about them," my father said over the dinner table, "is they're all named Mike."

The Italian kids were tough, by reputation, so discretion kept the fights to a minimum. They were athletes too, the guys, so they soon shared popularity with the tough incumbent boys. The girls likewise were accepted, at least by girls. To the hapless lot of boys, the entire tribe of females turned exotic in those final few years of grade school—large, womanly, intimidating. As the archdiocese achieved its integration between ethnic groups of schoolchildren, shepherding

43

them together for liturgical prayer every weekday at 7 a.m., the male children dreamed their own integration with the Amazonian opposite sex, and prayed for strength.

Thanks largely to St. John's, there even were black kids, so few they were forced to wear their distinctiveness like flowing robes, as if they were exchange students from Ghana. "Nigger" was a word for white ears only, but differences weren't exactly celebrated. A quiet girl named Nerina was told firmly by one of her teachers that her name had to be Noreen, precipitating an identity crisis that passed without reaching the courts or the newspapers. My mother, a beautiful person whom I lost before I was eight years old, sent a black classmate back to school, good-humoredly and gracefully, when I brought her home one lunchtime. This was Fountain Square in the 1950s, the athletic glory days of all-black Crispus Attucks High School, the same era Father Philip Berrigan was being transferred around by the Josephite order for trying to desegregate his parishes in the South.

In God's community, people kept to His business as it was laid out for them. Adults could choose from four masses on Sundays and two every weekday morning. They had confession on Saturday night and fish sticks and tomato soup on Fridays. They could give up beer and/or cigarettes during Lent. They could fit their spirituality in, you might say. For kids, however, faith kept no schedule. It hounded you day and night. The sisters kept up the daily rote drumbeat of the *Baltimore Catechism*. Out of their sight and hearing, the guys who could swear plagued you with their tantalizing talent. The guys who suggested we'd be better off as heathens, living it up and then getting a pass to Heaven because nobody had shown us the rules, haunted you with their unassailable subversive logic. And the girls were Hell on Earth.

The girls were fearsome when you were with them and when you

were not. They were occasions of sin, leading to impure thoughts, words, and deeds. If you wanted to receive the Holy Eucharist and die in a state of grace (should a passing motorist have a heart attack and his car veer onto the sidewalk and flatten you), you had to confess those thoughts, words, and deeds, all three.

Before adolescence, you could tell the anonymous silhouette behind the plastic screen that you'd spoken harshly to your sister and used God's name in vain ten times since your last confession. Three Our Fathers and five Hail Marys and you walked free, recharged with virtue. But in the long, long years between the onset of puberty and the self-licensing of adulthood, you had to confess to the sin of self-abuse, and keep track of the number of times, sometimes a mathematical challenge. By the lightness of his penance, you could sometimes tell that a particular priest wanted the youthful trespasser to give himself a break; but remarkably enough, there was less comfort in liberation than in meeting one's fallen nature on a Saturday evening, face to face in the feeble light of offertory candles, and sending it up in smoke.

In our time, fear and guilt are enjoying something of a comeback. The reactionary forces that treated us as Papist pagans when I was a child, suspicious of our refusal to enter the mainstream via the public schools, doubtful that John F. Kennedy wasn't getting his marching orders from Rome, extol Catholic schools nowadays as proud settlements in a jungle of state-subsidized ignorance and sloth. The Catlickers, as the pastor's children at Foursquare Tabernacle so vehemently called us from the safety of their yard, have traded places with the Puplickers. This is particularly strange to me because the principal reason my father sent me to Catholic school no longer exists. His theory was that you got a better education from the nuns because they had no families of their own to go home to and thus could devote all their energies to their pupils. Today, relatively few nuns teach, and they no longer live in communal quarters on the parish grounds.

We had nuns who were violent, nuns who were gentle, nuns who were both; nuns who were tolerant of *tempora et mores* and nuns who proclaimed the Blessed Virgin Mary must weep over women who paint their faces or walk down the street with a cigarette in their mouths or wear skirts that reveal their exact figure. Not to mention boys who went about in summer with their shirts off. Sister Mary Ephraim once walked into the boys' john, lined up three likely suspects in some incident of disorderly conduct, and slapped all their faces in a series of single sweeps, back and forth and back again, as Moe would do to Larry and Curly if he were after pain instead of laughs. This same anointed woman, so free with her dire right hand, also kept after me, well into high school, to raise my grades and consider going to college, something no one in my family ever had done.

My parents regarded the sisters as lawgivers, not to be questioned nor even consulted. My father never saw warrant even to enter the building in the years his five were in the nuns' custody. But toward the end of his life, when he was sour on about everything, he became possessed by this image of them as frustrated old maids and only grudgingly allowed them, now in their sensible slacks and sweaters, to visit him to give communion. He wasn't the romantic I am, and it hurt, knowing how he'd spoken of them, to hear the church women at his wake speaking of the honor of administering his viaticum—the final, departing eucharist. At the same time, I know I must be careful not to underestimate them; having been with more old men at the moment of God's summoning than I had, they probably knew all that I knew about his state of mind and heart, and much that I didn't.

Educated and sheltered, the Sisters of Providence were not looked to for advocacy or even empathy, but for rigor. There were sweet temperaments among them, and there were persimmons; but I don't remember a single hug against those black folds, heavy as stage curtains. In fact, it was pretty much taboo to touch their person. The girls clustered around the sisters in the schoolyard, politicking as their mothers and grandmothers had before them. The boys wondered if there were breasts under those starched white bibs. In my early years of school, the Sisters of Providence wore cardboard cowls around their faces that eliminated peripheral vision and allowed your buddies to make faces right alongside a teacher who was lecturing you, while you fought desperately to suppress that fatal smile. Later, they shrank those to visor size in the evolution toward laymen's dress. Sister Thomas, the principal, was bareheaded and wearing a business suit when I met her a quarter century after graduation, in St. Francis Hospital, where she was working as a chaplain and my father was dying. Impulsively, I framed her face with my hands as I joked about the old days, a stage of our lives that she seemed to have relegated far more neatly than I.

There are two extremes of untroubled faith—evangelical fire and Catholic inertia. One day when I was home from college I had a visit from an insurance salesman who'd been bugging me for a couple years to buy a starter life policy. We went to the corner to discuss it over coffee, and he commenced to ask some questions about college life. He wanted to know what sorts of things kids talked about. All sorts of things, I told him.

Do they ever talk about Jesus Christ? he asked me.

Uh, sure. This was the '60s, after Vatican II. Jesus the original revolutionary, etc. Jesus was cool.

That wasn't what he meant. He meant the regular thing. The insurance salesman had been saved, and he wanted to know how receptive I was to being saved.

As far as I was concerned, the good news he was bringing was that he had lost interest in selling me insurance. The bad news was that I couldn't get rid of him simply by explaining that I already had religion.

45

It's strange how they never hesitate to approach Catholics. If he had the same Jesus I had, why was he wasting his proselytizing on me?

If I had the same Jesus he had, on the other hand, why was I uneasy?

Mission work was not for us, not then. Evangelizing was done in Africa and on Indian reservations. On the Fountain, we made our own Christians right at home, their production being the only justification for carnal pleasure; and we baptized them when they were still pink and hairless. Our harvest was bountiful. At its peak—my years—St. Pat's had five hundred pupils, three priests, and a two-story apartment building filled with nuns. Because the Sunday collection was so large and the sisters worked for room and board, tuition was modest even by that day's standards; and if you were poor, you just told them so and went for free. My family enrolled all its five without paying a nickel, unless you count the dollar my father threw into the collection basket every Sunday. The alternative—public school—was unacceptable to the family and the parish alike, and that was that.

Being poor in St. Pat's in the 1950s was not the same as being poor to the Berrigan brothers or Dorothy Day or the operators of Casa Maria halfway house in Milwaukee, where I went to college in radicalism's heyday. Being poor wasn't showing the face of Christ and shaming the economic system. Being poor was being sent to the lavatory to scrub your face, being kept in from recess because your coat had no buttons, being told—discreetly—that you looked as though nobody owned you. When it came time to deliver your Favorite Christmas Present speech, you could try to convey the subtle glamour of a new sweatshirt, or you could claim it was a Bulova watch that you kept forgetting at home. Then, you'd confess the lie. The sacrament of penance has since been supplanted by the sacrament of reconciliation, in which the sinner would not list his lies but rather would discuss with his priest the burdens of materialism and worldly status, and the intrinsic virtue of living simply.

St. Patrick's has a mission to "read from the book of the poor" now. It is not the heart of a community of working-class and middle-class Catholics. Those people followed the freeways that lacerated a dispensable neighborhood to nourish the suburbs and the suburban churches. Today, St. Patrick's and its remnant are part of a neighborhood of poor non-Catholics with many needs some of which would not be met except for the means and grace of the Catholic parish. Its classrooms are serving as a homeless shelter. Its nuns' quarters are used by an agency helping single pregnant women. It offers two Spanish masses a week for a new generation of immigrants. Though it has no school, and no resident priest, and no convent, St. Patrick's is not diminished.

St. Patrick's is not diminished, but it is gone, and we miss it whether or not we mourn it. In 1961, on a Sunday afternoon too glorious to have happened at random, the parish held one of its most memorable May crownings of all time. With the big church filled with families and afire with flashbulbs, the student body marching through the columned aisles chanting lovely archaic poetry to the Blessed Virgin Mary against the ringing engine of the pipe organ, even boys gave in to the grandeur of Michelangelo's brass-and-marble Church of Rome. Even boys who were forced to borrow their fathers' short, wide painted silk ties from the prewar era, their fathers' ballooning wrinkled white shirts.

All the spectacle of the procession was prologue to a perilous drama, in which an eighth-grade girl of the nuns' choosing tiptoed up a miniature stepladder before the packed church and placed the flowered laurel atop a statue whose bowed plaster head she barely

46

could reach. My sister had the honor, in this great year of our ascendancy, this first year of a Roman Catholic President, and she did the unthinkable and inevitable: She bumped the statue. The congregation gasped as the sacred effigy rocked forward and back, forward and back, before settling safely in position on its pedestal. God may watch as a sparrow falls or a nation is incinerated, but there are some catastrophes that can find no place within His—or His loving mother's—inscrutable sufferance.

> Ho-ly Mar-y, pra-ay for u-us
> Holy Mother of Go-od, pra-ay for u-us.
> Holy Virgin of Virgins . . .
> Mother of Good Counsel . . .
> Mirror of Justice . . .
> Vessel of Honor . . .
> Tower of David . . .
> Comforter of the Afflicted . . .
> Queen of Peace, Pray for us.

Fear worked well as a prod and guide through the tunnels of religious formation, but it also could steer us away from some of them. Fear of the *Confiteor* sidetracked me. Most able-bodied males, even the least venturesome and least pious, enlisted in the legions of altar boys needed for all those masses. One or two served at each of the small early morning liturgies, four at a Sunday high mass—lots of masses and lots of Latin. The first thing you had to do was memorize the *Confiteor* ("I confess to almighty God") in the Latin, and stand ready to be tested at the first meeting. I choked. I told my dad I didn't want to do it. He skipped an opportunity to give a push, and I was left to watch my friends and wait around for them afterwards, just as I did in sports. The difference, of course, was that when it happened in baseball, I went home and cried.

Parishes choose whether or not to have altar boys now, and the altar boys aren't only boys, and they don't have to learn Latin, and they don't get cut from the team. What's the bottom line of all this—less or more traditional morality?

Tradition bends to the world and the flesh. My childhood, filled with funerals, was set to the tolling of that great bell in the Spanish Baroque tower over Fountain Square. The knell, it turns out, was for a way of life. Father Thomas Fields, a veteran of World War II who presided over mass and drove about in long black Buicks and commanded our instant standing attention when he strode into classrooms, died in 1964, his fifteenth year as pastor of St. Patrick's. He and his peers have not been replaced. The mission lands are yielding up ordinations, but priests in the United States are outnumbered by parishes, and they are past middle age on the average, those who remain, those who haven't left to get married. Families have risen economically, and have fewer children, and are less inclined to encourage a son and a daughter into the religious life. Nor is it scandalous any longer when someone joins and then leaves.

Cosmas Raimondi, who came to St. Pat's as a first-grader in the Holy Rosary invasion, became an activist priest at St. Thomas and then at Holy Cross, losing his Honda Civic to the Internal Revenue Service over a refusal to pay that part of his taxes that went to nuclear weaponry. He was the new breed of democracy-minded priest, the brother in jeans succeeding the patriarch in the collar; and now he's working in the mental health field—like many former priests and nuns, continuing to minister through a helping profession. When I spoke with him ten years after his ten-year career as a priest,

47

I mentioned my father's old tenet about the full-time dedication of religious personnel. He smiled. "The church took care of you," he said. "They made sure you had nothing else to think about and you could spend all your time on your work. But the price of that was the loss of your personal life. There may be some who can give themselves completely to an institution, but I couldn't. And until the church comes up with a way to provide that security without taking away part of your personality, it will lose a lot of good people."

Cos Raimondi attends an Episcopal church in his neighborhood. On clerical celibacy and other issues, he doesn't believe the Vatican has been correct or honest, and he cannot picture himself in the pew at St. Thomas or Holy Cross, at least for now. Other former priests and nuns have been likewise critical of the hierarchy, but have remained part of the new diffuse leadership of the American church, the engaged proprietary laity. From where I stand, the difference between them and him is all but imperceptible compared to the difference between the church of my childhood and the church of my middle age. Their Christianity and mine is looking like the Early Church, before hierarchy, before all these edifices with iron doors a child running late for morning mass needs two hands to open. The complication is, the iron doors are my personal Early Church, from which I could not walk free if I wanted to.

As an only son, not to mention a non-altar boy, I wasn't a good bet for the priesthood, but I was a prospect somehow, driven, along with several classmates, to St. Meinrad Seminary in southern Indiana one summer day by Father Gerry Burkert, a youthful assistant to Father Fields. The idea was to persuade any or all of us in this elect of eighth-graders to enroll in the Latin School, a now-defunct high school on our own Southside that prepared youth for

ascent to St. Meinrad. Our interest was more immediate. We wanted to see if a priest was like everybody else on his day off, and we wanted to test his tolerance for our gossip and gripes. "You're wishing evil on people," he finally admonished us for our croaks and snarls of incipient manhood, but since we always spoke like this, we had to wonder whether we offended Jesus practically all the time or practically never. There were too many guys who could talk about your mama for some of them not to end up in everlasting life, and in the priesthood.

Though I've admired certain priests more than any other men, I've never quite pictured myself in such a station. When the moment was upon me, I was in awe. The effect of St. Meinrad, that majestic monument to German settlers' hope and nostalgia, was to underscore the smallness of the world of children of the big Irish church.

Its twin spires and sandstone battlements rising from the green hills like an apparition from another millennium, St. Meinrad was and is a seminary, a church, a Benedictine monastery, a publishing business, and a town, among other things. I would write about it thirty years later as a dream and a verity, a confounding specimen of rural and traditional persistence, as disdainful of time as the swords and the Latin. I gave more thought to joining its scholars as a family man who had seen the realm than I did as a lonely twelve-year-old anxious to beat Hell. And yet . . .

How full of grace that afternoon was. I threw up at lunch from the excitement; I learned that seminarians shoot pool on their journey toward perfection, and I rode home with a mental imprint of those towers in the country that has stayed with me ever since as an intimation of how far you can travel from Shelby Street.

The Blood Tie
Dan Wakefield

I realized the journey that brought me home to Boston from Hollywood had skipped a crucial part—perhaps the hardest part of all. Five years after I'd settled back into my old neighborhood on Beacon Hill and returned to my religious roots when I joined King's Chapel, I still had not made peace with the home I was born and grew up in. I'd avoided Indianapolis for many years, only going back when circumstances forced me, even then returning in the style of a thief in the night, not telling anyone except the few people I had to see. In the fall of 1985 I looked uneasily at a headline announcing a talk I was scheduled to give at the Indianapolis-Marion County Public Library: "Dan Wakefield—A Prodigal Son Returns." I was going to try again.

When my flight out of Boston was delayed I began to get nervous. The last time I'd boarded a plane to make a public appearance in Indianapolis I never got there. That was fifteen years before, when my leaving-home first novel was published in 1970. It was called *Going All the Way* and a lot of people in Indianapolis who read it thought I had gone too far. Phone calls and letters and secondhand rumors (as well as painfully censorious silence from old friends) had made it clear there was a lot of hostility toward me and my book back home in Indiana. Some people (mostly ones I barely knew) firmly believed I had exposed their most intimate secrets or those of their wives or daughters, and threatened to wreak vengeance. Others felt I had cast aspersions on their community and its values, the place of my own birth and upbringing. All this made me wish I had followed an early anticipation of such misunderstanding and set the damn book in Cleveland.

There was also disapproval in some quarters from people unaccustomed or unsympathetic to the manners of current fiction, who felt that my frank use of "language" describing sexual experiences and fantasies was shocking and immoral. At the twenty-fifth reunion of my high school class, which I was too chicken to attend, my old classmate Dick Lugar, then mayor of Indianapolis, got a big laugh when he said he had read my novel, after receiving it through the mail "in a plain brown wrapper."

My publisher's publicity director had assured me I was being oversensitive when I didn't want to go back home for book promotion, especially after an Indianapolis television station offered to pay all expenses for me to come and be interviewed on their talk show. I grudgingly agreed to do it, even though discomforting omens warned me otherwise. That morning of departure was foggy, with rain, and someone in the office of my publisher had clipped out a picture for me from the *New York Daily News* that showed a woman accused of murdering her boyfriend being led out of a brownstone by armed police. I asked what the story had to do with me and was told to look closer at the picture. The accused murderess was shielding her face from the cameras with a book—it was a copy of *Going All the Way*. Did my novel promote mayhem in people? I laughed nervously, downed a morning drink, and went to the airport.

The flight was scheduled to go to Indianapolis, Kansas City, and San Francisco, but we made an emergency landing in Pittsburgh because of a bomb threat to TWA from a caller who said, "That plane will never get to Indianapolis." Quivering in the concrete blockhouse where passengers huddled while the aircraft was searched for bombs, I told my story to an FBI man who said he didn't believe the threat was linked to anything like a novel or its author–they thought it had to do with a stewardess and a broken date–but when I confided my fears to a woman passenger who taught high school in Bloomington, Indiana, she said, "I've heard people talk about your book, and if I were you I wouldn't go back either." The wail of police sirens rang in my mind from the end of a popular song of the season called "Indiana Wants Me." How many signs and portents did I need? I joined those who took the airline's offer to return to New York instead of continuing the interrupted flight and told the publicity director over a stiff brandy that Thomas Wolfe was right: "You can't go home again."

In the decade that followed I practiced Wolfe's preachment. I only went back once to Indianapolis on a quick trip to see my parents (pledging them not to tell anyone of my arrival), preferring to send them tickets every year to visit me wherever I was at the time. I justified that arrangement because it seemed to be less emotion-charged for all concerned. I lost track of dear friends from high school I'd kept in touch with over the years (the ones who stayed home, not my fellow migrants like Hickman in Tampa or Ted "The Horse" in New York, with whom I not only shared the experience of Indiana but also of leaving it), fearing they felt I'd betrayed them. The book was seen by some as the final cap to my earlier transgressions of going East and becoming an alleged pinko, bohemian, beatnik, hippie (to match the changing times and styles), a middle-aged divorced man without children, a turncoat against the values and beliefs I'd been nurtured on while growing up, making me seem a sort of Indiana Benedict Arnold, betrayer of my own roots. (As if this image weren't bad enough, I'd heard rumors out of Indianapolis over the years alleging me to be at different times a drug addict and a homosexual, which added to my other alleged sins might make me the first Hoosier-gay-pinko-junkie-pornographer.)

When I went home in 1980 for the funerals of my father and mother I was surprised and relieved and unutterably grateful to see old high school friends I hadn't talked with in more than a decade–some I had not even seen since high school graduation thirty years before. When I flew in for my father's funeral, having just broken up with Eve and feeling more alone than I ever remembered, I put on my best suit and smile and stationed myself at the front of the antiseptic room with my father lying in a coffin behind me and wondered how the hell I was going to get through it.

A handsome man with distinguished white hair came toward me and I dutifully stuck out my hand and said, "Hello, I'm Dan Wakefield." The man smiled and said in a voice and accent I knew and loved, "It's Harpie." My best friend from high school. I remembered once doing a story for *Esquire* on Happy Chandler when he came out of retirement to run again for governor of Kentucky. He had gone to a funeral at which the father of the family, an old friend and ally, came up and threw his arms around the candidate and said, "Good God, Governor, there's no one on earth I'd rather see." That's how I felt when I recognized Harpie, though in Indiana we men don't embrace and express emotion the way they do unashamedly to our South, so I simply shook hands with my old friend and said, "Thanks."

At those times of death the support of friends from home was the most saving grace I was given. No matter what some may have disapproved of about my life or what rumors they had heard of it, those friends were there in that experience of grief because I had shared with them that precious era that Jerry Burton, my friend since kindergarten, described in a letter as "those wonderful heart-breaking days when we lived so much of our lives, in such a few short years." Even had I been the first Hoosier gay-pinko-junkie-pornographer, I also was, more importantly, one of them, and they were there to stand by me. There is a loyalty of place as deep as blood, something in and of the flat, true heart of the Midwest, a slowly grown sentiment born of the very plainness of the land, something solid that takes root and holds, and that sticks forever. I saw that in the old friends from home who came at those difficult times, so many years later, and I loved them for it.

Something held me back, though, from returning to re-establish those old friendships after my parents had died. It seemed as though there still was some kind of invisible barrier between me and Indianapolis that I couldn't manage to cross. I didn't go back again until four years after my mother's and father's funerals, but even then I still didn't tell my old friends I was coming. In my old thief-in-the-night manner, I kept my trip a secret from almost everyone I knew in Indianapolis except my Cousin Paula, who I knew I could trust not to let anyone know I was coming.

Maybe my reluctance was simply due to a revival of old guilt, for I was going back to show my writer-producer friend Don Devlin around the city to scout locations for a movie version he wanted to make of *Going All the Way*. Even though the film he hoped to produce was an "update" of the story from the 1950s to the 1980s and bore little resemblance to the original, I still feared the project might upset people again, reopening old wounds. On the other hand, I'd rationalized that Don's movie was not really a film of the novel. Like the movie version of my novel *Starting Over*, it would only use the book as what the writer of that script described as a "launching pad" for the movie. Nevertheless, I didn't want to open the whole can of worms by bringing up the subject to old friends in Indianapolis. I told myself to stop worrying and just enjoy the trip.

One of the worst blizzards in recent Indiana history covered the city the week I was scheduled to meet my writer-producer friend in Indianapolis that February of 1984. Don called me in Boston from Hollywood and asked if we ought to postpone the trip, but I wanted to do it and get it over with. He and I shivered and slid around a frozen Indianapolis for several days, enjoying good conversation about potential locations if he got the project into production and decided to do the shooting there, which he realized wasn't essential to the new version of the story.

The Sunday morning before going back to Boston, I decided to visit my parents' graves. I wanted some kind of reconciliation with them, and even though I had prayed for it, I wanted to do something else, specific and tangible, to try to bring it about. I knew that the bones of my mother and father were in the ground, and I had no illusion their incarnated bodies were floating around somewhere in the atmosphere, yet I'd sensed emanations of their essence, or whatever unknown, unnamable quality it was Aunt Ollie had sensed and sometimes communicated with in her own rapport with the "spirits" of those who had left this earthly life. Once in the year after my mother's death, when I had just made a decision that troubled me and in fact turned out very badly, I clearly heard my mother crying, as close and "real" as if she were in the same room.

I had never visited anyone's grave before, and never been able to understand what seemed the barbaric practice of standing over a plot of ground that covered the bones of the dead. Now it seemed at least a symbolic spot for paying respects to whatever manifestation of the deceased still remained in this realm of the living, even if it only remained in the heart or soul of the mourner. Whatever the case may have been, I was nervous. Cousin Paula had drawn me a map showing my parents' plots in Crown Hill Cemetery, but I got lost in that immense, eerie landscape, made more stark and somber by the covering of ice and snow. No other visitors had come to pay respects on such a bone-chilling morning, nor were any officials or attendants in sight. I was not made more comfortable by the observation that I seemed to be the only living soul in the huge, otherworldly kingdom of the cemetery. I was alone with my parents and the rest of the dead.

I knelt in the snow beside my parents' graves, feeling cold and discomforted. I said the Twenty-third Psalm, going through it pretty briskly, muttered a request for forgiveness for not more freely expressing my love to them in their lifetime, then shifted on my knees. The layer of snow crunched beneath me. I wondered if the earth might open and swallow me, sucking me into a grave beside my parents. That had been a painful point of contention with us. On a trip to New York in the mid-seventies my mother blithely told me the "good news" that she and my father had just purchased their cemetery plots at Crown Hill, and that there happened to be bargain sale, "three for the price of two," on grave sites, so they had got one for me right beside them.

"No!" I shouted. "No way!" We were having lunch in the main restaurant of the New York Hilton, where I had put them up on that visit, and other tourists at nearby tables turned and stared at my unseemly outburst. I felt an awful panic, a fear that my parents had found a way to trap me at last, to keep me "home" with them through eternity, thus negating my noble escape and establishment of independence! My mother answered my spontaneous rejection of their generous offer by pointing out, "You have to be buried someplace!" I denied this, explaining I wanted to be cremated, but my mother, whose hearing difficulty always became more acute with information she didn't like, cupped a hand to her ear and asked what I'd said. With heart pounding, I threw down my napkin, stood up, and shouted:

"I want to be cremated and have my ashes scattered on Beacon Hill!"

The entire population of the large dining room turned toward me as my father heaved one of his heartrending sighs and I sank back down in my chair, trembling. When I got back to Boston I went to my lawyer and made up the first "last will and testament" of my life, spelling out my wishes for interment in no uncertain terms.

All that came rushing back to me as I knelt on the cracking ice beside my parents' graves, perhaps on the very plot they had purchased for me. I bade them a hasty farewell and clambered up from the frozen ground, slipping and sliding to the car. I jumped in and slammed the door, jammed the key in the ignition, and prepared to turn the key to escape to my airline flight, whose time of departure was drawing close. The key wouldn't turn. It wouldn't budge. Not at all. I frantically searched my pockets for other keys, but this was it. I took it out and stuck it in again, with no better results. I flung open the door and scrambled out of the car, calling for help. There of course was no one. On that freezing Sunday morning the place was quite literally dead. I felt as if some kind of force field had formed around me, a trap that had sprung from my parents' graves to hold me there with them. I could feel the anger and power of my mother and father, their sense of disappointment in what they interpreted as rejection by their only son. I could feel their presence. I started to run.

I ran as fast as I could up the winding paths of the cemetery toward a large mausoleum that seemed to be the focal point of the whole place. Part of my mind saw myself from an aerial view, a lone man running through a deserted, snow-covered cemetery, past the whitened statues, the memorial crosses and blocks of marble—a figure in a frieze from an outtake of a Bergman film. The rest of my consciousness was filled with pure, unreasoning panic.

There was a guard on duty in an office in the mausoleum, and he came out and tried to get my borrowed engine started but had no better luck than I did. The key simply wouldn't budge. Back at the mausoleum office I called Cousin Paula, who came with a neighbor and was not able to turn the key to start the car herself, though she said she couldn't understand it; they had had that car for years and nothing like this ever happened before. The neighbor took me to the airport and I just made the plane to Boston. When I got home safe I called Cousin Paula to learn that her husband had gone back with her to the car that afternoon and the key worked perfectly, no problem at all, and Jim couldn't believe that neither I, nor the cemetery guard, nor Paula, nor her neighbor had been able to get it to turn.

The memory of those previous "prodigal son" efforts I had made didn't give me lots of confidence for the new attempt when I went back for the library talk in the autumn of 1985. When my flight out of Boston was delayed I got even more nervous. I tried to reassure myself by thinking about the church retreat on "Reconciliation" I'd gone on the previous weekend, where we'd studied the story of the prodigal son. Surely that gave me the best kind of preparation and blessing for this latest try. As I waited for my flight to take off, I knew I was ready to renew old ties with the high school friends I hoped to see, but I wished now I didn't have to do it as part of a public appearance. I'd agreed to speak at the library as part of their series of Conversations with Indiana Authors, and to help promote the event with interviews on local television and in the press.

What if some of those irate fathers or husbands who were angered when *Going All the Way* was published came to my talk to avenge what they imagined were personal slurs on their loved ones; or those who felt my novel had insulted their entire community and way of life? What if they hurled tomatoes or eggs, or at least hostile, heckling questions?

"I see myself on this return like the aging warrior, wrinkled and weathered, with feathers turned to gray, raising a hand in blessing and saying, 'I come in peace.'" That's what I said in an interview about my upcoming lecture for the Indianapolis Public Library newsletter, but that didn't guarantee how other people would see me. Dear God, may I really find reconciliation. I twisted in my seat as the plane began to taxi down the runway for take-off, lifting into thick, gray skies and hurtling west toward the heartland.

The next day I was shooting baskets with Harpie in his backyard. The smack and echo of the basketball on the grassy ground, the feel of its grainy skin on my fingers, thud of the banked shot against the wooden backboard, then a run for the rebound, breath coming clean and sharp in the chest—all of this was deeply reassuring and made me feel this trip back home was not only safe but right. Harpie and I were playing ball in the falling sun and shadow of a late October afternoon, with the dizzying fresh perfume of new-mown hay coming over the long flat fields, the whole of it creating a full harmony of home, a blood- and bone-deep rhythm of casual order, a ritual I relaxed into like a warm bath or a deep bed of the most complete imaginable comfort, the comfort of deepest inner self, of soul.

I was home, as I had been, and would be—now, then, again, it was all one. Time seemed fluid rather than fixed, not linear but spiraling, mysterious and luminous beyond our grasp.

53

Playing basketball in Harpie's backyard, I was (am) a child, boy, gray-haired man, old coot I've yet to become.

The sunset that evening was one of the most spectacular displays of intense essences of colors—fiery, molten golds and reds—I can ever remember seeing, more brilliant even than the ones I had witnessed in the clear air of the Caribbean. Harpie said the sunsets were often like that this time of year in the farm country north of town because of a kind of dust that gets into the air from the harvesting of the corn. It acts as a filter that intensifies the light. It made me think of the word "glory" as in "The glory of the Lord shone round about them." (I realized it did more often than we think, but we're too preoccupied to notice.)

Our high school is unabashedly called "glorious Shortridge" in its anthem and we sang it that night at the tops of our lungs at the party at Harpie's, several dozen men and women who more than three decades before had befriended one another in a bond that seemed as strong and real in our early fifties as it had been in our teens. After I accepted the invitation to speak at the library I had called Harpie, whom I hadn't seen since my mother's funeral, nor sat down for a real talk with in more than twenty years, and asked if he'd mind getting some of the old gang together the night before my public performance. Realizing what a presumptuous request this was made me feel nervous, but as soon as Harpie started talking about it, going over names of people we'd like to see, the whole thing seemed as natural now as it had when we planned such parties back then, in high school.

Everyone looked so much the same except for whitening hair that I had the eerie feeling we had all gone back from the future to our high school selves for a party that required everyone to wear a gray wig. The talk was much the same—we spoke of favorite teachers like Dorothy and Abie and joked about "Krazy Kate," who

enacted history by sticking her foot in the wastebasket and shouting, "I claim this land for Spain!" Bugsy spontaneously gave an account of the game with Withrow of Cincinnati we went into undefeated; he was playing quarterback and thought he heard the referee's whistle while he had the ball so he set it down on the grass and an enemy player jumped on it and the ref said, "First down, Withrow," and they went in and scored and beat us by a touchdown. "I know I heard that whistle," he said. I knew it too; and I couldn't believe the game he described was played any longer ago than the past weekend.

Like most of us there, I was drinking no more than Diet Coke and I know the warmth and trust we felt was not just a boozy illusion. Linda said her own kids never understood what the big deal was about her high school. Everyone agreed their own children had not enjoyed the special sort of bond we shared that still drew us together with a sense of loyalty and love no less than it had been three decades and more before. As I talked to Linda, Jerry, Janet, Ferdie, Pat, and the others I had such a sense of relief and trust that I got the deep feeling that these people, their faces and voices and love, this place we were born and grew up in—this was "real," and the rest of my life, the part since I left home to go to college and stay on living in the East, all that was "the dream." I used to think it was just the other way around. I remembered Eugene O'Neill's concept of youth and middle age being the "strange interlude" between childhood and old age, and wondered if that was part of this sudden sensation I had at the party with the old gang.

The next night at the library I announced that I wanted to dedicate the evening to the memory of my mother and father. I felt it was not just a gesture of piety but a true declaration of my love that would somehow be communicated. I was addressing my parents as well as the audience when I explained some of the deep feelings I had about this place and its people, feelings most brilliantly articulated by Eudora Welty in her essay "Place in Fiction": "There may come to be new places in our lives that are second spiritual homes—closer to us in some ways, perhaps, than our original homes. But the home tie is the blood tie. And had it meant nothing to us, any other place thereafter would have meant less, and we would carry no compass inside ourselves to find home, ever, anywhere at all. We would not even guess what we had missed."

No hecklers were in the audience, only friends and readers and old neighbors from back before high school. I did not quote anything from *Going All the Way* but closed my talk by reading the nostalgic short story "Autumn Full of Apples" that poured from me like a love song to home twenty years before on a bright fall day in New England: "We cheered because we thought we had outrun everything—the day and the season and the year and all years—and we would never be caught by them, never pulled anywhere beyond this sixteenth sweet-and-sour apple autumn, cursing and kissing as if we had invented them both." And there we were in the library, "caught" and pulled ahead by time, but circling back in it, too, feeling those sixteen-year-old selves alive and vivid in memory real as flesh.

I now saw a new dimension to the great key line that expresses the moment the prodigal son decides to go home: "he came to himself." It meant on this trip of my own return a coming to terms not only of acceptance of a true inner self but also of the place in which that self was born, took root, was nourished, and grew.

I did not have the nerve to go back to visit my parents' graves on that trip, not wanting to risk any conflicting feeling to spoil the tremendous spirit of reconciliation with home, as well as—I hoped and prayed—with my mother and father. I went back to visit their graves on a trip to Indianapolis the following spring. On a day of soft sunlight and gusty, clean breezes I knelt again beside them. The weather inside me had changed too, in part because I felt a real reconciliation had taken place when I honored my parents in public and also accepted in some deeper way the love for them I had buried so long in angry denial. There was an aura of calm around their graves now, and I felt my parents' presence again, but this time with peace, like a blessing. I took it with me and prayed to leave them mine, with love.

HIGH SCHOOL SPIRIT
Barbara Shoup

The summer before I left for college, I worked second shift at a map factory. Every afternoon at two o'clock, I set out to catch the bus that would take me there. It was a long walk. It was always hot, I was always tired. I felt nauseous on the bus, I rode with my eyes closed. When I got off, I dragged myself across a busy street, across a little park, into the factory, where it felt cool—but only for a moment. Promptly at three, I punched the time clock and walked into the rhythmic din. Big steel machines lined the narrow path I followed back to the area where I worked. Maps were spitting out of them, stacking up; beautiful pastel maps of places I longed to see.

My job was packing. I stood on the assembly line with a dozen or so sad, tired women, most of them the age of my mother, lifting globes and atlases from the flat wooden trolleys and placing them in the boxes going by on the conveyor belt. My back and shoulders hurt. I felt as if the concrete floor were coming right up through my feet. I watched the clock, watched the high windows darken to night. Soon, I told myself, your real life will begin. But I could not really believe it.

Years later, smack in the middle of this real life, I stand with my high school writing students in a map factory in Indianapolis. There is the same hum and throb and clatter of machinery, the same smell of print and glue and paper. For just an instant, there is the claustrophobia of that distant summer, the longing. Then, watching my students absorb this new world, there is the jolt of pleasure that comes to me sometimes when I am with them, that almost alarming joy. The pretty pastel rosettes that workers feed into round molds delight them. One mold is cool and they are allowed to touch the inside of it, to feel the cavities that make mountains rise on the surface of each globe. There are stacks of half-globes everywhere.

"Hey, these would make cool bike helmets," someone says, and everybody laughs.

Hundreds of finished worlds have been sprayed with lacquer and are suspended above us, a whole universe. When they are dry, the ball-poker rolls them down from their tracks with his big stick, like God. Smitten with words, my young writers love this job name: "ball-poker." They love everything they see.

What I love is to be with them. The shock of the ordinary world seen as they see it, fresh and new. The true response which they have not yet learned to hide. There, standing among them, surrounded by miniature worlds, I think, This is what church must feel like to some people.

I was not raised in any church; I had virtually no religious training as a child. One of the worst experiences of my girlhood was a week I spent at a Christian camp when I was in junior high. I had gone out of desperation, to protect my interest in a fickle friendship with a girl I'd worshipped since grade school, and she ditched me upon arrival, as I had feared she would. All alone in a strange place, I went to meals, to recreational activities, to Bible study like a zombie. But even in such misery, even trying my best to be invisible, I could not help but voice the questions that invariably popped into my head. *Were Adam and Eve cave people? If your wife or husband dies when you are very young and you remarry, who will you be with in heaven?*

More and deeper questions plagued me in the late sixties and early seventies, when, as a young mother, I joined the Lutheran church, feeling an obligation to offer my two daughters the religious foundation that I had not had. *How can I feel that I, a woman, truly belong here,when everything we sing or speak is He? Why do we send so much money to missionaries overseas when there are families six blocks away from our church who desperately need our help? Why are there no black people in our congregation? Why won't good Christians take a stand about the war in Vietnam?*

I was too literal a person for organized religion, I decided. I couldn't find much connection between what the church taught and what it practiced. I couldn't and still can't fathom the kind of personal relationship with Jesus that so many Christians describe. Nor can I make sense of or find solace in the promise of redemption. I hate the idea that we are all sinners, bad at the core, and only Jesus can save us. I could believe in the concept of one life on earth as random, meaningless, a quirk of biology, before I could believe in a father-god who creates us in love, yet doles out such disparate earthly existences.

So I left the church and set out on my own spiritual path, cobbling a personal religion that better suited the person I am still hoping to become. Be Here Now. Look, question, learn. Remember paradox. Never lie to yourself.

I believe in Vermeer's "View of Delft." In Tim O'Brien's "Lives of the Dead," which begins: "But this too is true: stories can save us." In Kurt Vonnegut's advice to a nursery full of newborns via his character, Elliot Rosewater: "Goddamnit, you've got to be kind." And I believe in my young writers. They crack open the world I thought I knew. Unfailingly, in the strangest ways, they drive lessons I thought I'd already learned deeper and deeper inside me.

I've been fascinated the last few years by my students who are devout Christians, whose spiritual lives inform the work we do together. Where does this faith come from, I wonder? Will it last? Some, I think, are surely influenced by the various ways in which contemporary Christian churches market faith to teenagers. Youth group activities like skiing and camping, mission trips to communities from Appalachia to South America appeal to the their yearning to belong. Christian music festivals make faith cool. Last year, NPR's *Morning Edition* interviewed some of the thousands of teenagers who had converged on Washington, D.C., for a weekend of worship and witness. There was much laughter and shouting in the background, the heavy thump of bass. Earnest, breathless teenagers spoke of the inspiration they felt gathered with so many others of like minds. One boy declared, "Yeah, we're moshing for Jesus."

I saw them in my mind's eye—flannel-shirted boys with shaved heads and earrings; girls in ripped jeans with pre-Raphaelite hair—lost in the music, and I wondered, What would Jesus think of a bunch of teenagers careening around a mosh pit, writhing and flailing in His name?

Writing this now, I hear an edge of disdain in my words, and I stop and try to understand how I really feel about Christianity, remember that anything I say about the world has some effect on the young writers I teach. I count on them to keep me honest, both in my life in my work. I am humbled by the way they reveal their true selves to me. Often, I am flooded in their presence by what I have only ever been able to name as love. I would never willfully hurt them.

So do I delete that cynical reference to moshing for Jesus when I know that some of them may very well have moshed for

57

Jesus themselves? And what about thoughts I've had about the Happening, a twice-yearly Christian youth gathering that I know a number of my students have found deeply sustaining? An ecumenical weekend of peace and love, the Happening seems tailor-made for the children of the children of the sixties. Upon arriving Friday evening, participants receive a dozen or so letters from people they know and some they have never met, expressing pleasure that they have come to celebrate the life of Jesus. Telling them that they are loved. All weekend they participate in spiritual activities designed to bring them closer to each other and to Christ.

It is a good thing for so many of them, I know. Lots of these kids come from broken or troubled families; some have parents whose love is—or seems to them to be—contingent upon their academic and athletic success. Some deal with alcoholism, drug addiction, sexual confusion. They are searching for something to believe in, to rely on, and I remind myself of an E.M. Forster quote that I love: "Only connect."

But I cannot quiet the stubborn, questioning voice inside me. What good is a weekend of amorphous, unconditional love and compassion if it doesn't cause every single one of my students who experienced it to come to school on Monday, instantly notice the troubled, friendless classmate among them, and invite her along to the Abbey, where they spend endless hours drinking coffee, journaling, talking about Life? How does this weekend's Happening balance with the activities of the weekend before, which for some included gathering at a friend's empty house to drink themselves into oblivion?

These, of course, aren't questions of faith, but of action. And they certainly do not apply to the lives of all the Christian teenagers I know. The best of these young people live according to Christ's teachings as completely and intelligently as any human

being could; some have had the kind of life experiences from which a deep, complex religious faith is forged. They spoke from their hearts about what they believed; they thoughtfully considered the questions I asked them. I should attend Open Table some Sunday evening, several of them told me—a fledgling congregation of Disciples of Christ that they are helping to establish. Despite—no, *because* of—my dread of group spiritual experiences, it seemed only right for me go.

When I arrive at the little chapel, people are milling around, amused, waiting for the two kids in charge of tonight's service to return from the grocery store, where they've gone in a rush, having realized that they've forgotten about providing for Communion. One of my students introduces me to a kind-looking woman who, along with two other women, ordained pastors in the Disciples of Christ, were instrumental in beginning the new church. Her sincere welcome unnerves me a bit, and I let her know, awkwardly, that I'm writing about the spiritual lives of teenagers and I've come tonight to observe. It's a wonderful thing that's happening here, she tells me. What a surprise, what a pleasure it is to her that the congregation has turned out to be made up of so many young people.

In fact, of the twenty or so people here tonight, most of them are teenage girls. They're dressed comfortably in jeans or gypsy dresses, one in black "Goth" attire. There's a lot of laughing and hugging going on, spirited recountings of the weekend's adventures. Then the two kids who are to lead the worship tonight burst in, red-faced from the cold, bearing a loaf of bread and a bottle of grape juice, which they set on the altar, and it is time to begin.

I sit alone in a back pew, notebook in hand, scribbling impressions. *Cozy chapel, red carpet, bread in aluminum pie pan. Braids, black beret, bowler hat. Pearl Jam tee-shirt. White spindly neck.*

Announcements are made: The Park Manor Christian Church, an African-American congregation in Chicago, has learned of them and is including them in their prayers. Next Sunday, the Week of Compassion begins, a time to respond to the troubled people around the globe. In Nicaragua, for example, there is 65 percent unemployment, and there is a plan afoot to help the Disciples of Christ clergy working there to survive by sending farm animals. Unable to support themselves through church resources, they will raise and butcher the animals to make a living, thus allowing them to continue their ministry for Christ. Two weeks from tonight, there will be a pot-luck dinner and a meeting afterwards to begin work on a mission statement and a brochure that will describe what Open Table is.

Business concluded, it is time for the passing of the peace, a custom which never fails to make me feel like a child under the watchful eyes of her parents, directed to be nice. Clearly, though, that is not the way the young people here feel about it. The ritual takes a while, for many of them get up and move around the room, embracing one another and the adults among them, offering words of love and support.

There is no sermon, just a gospel reading—First Corinthians 8:1-13—and a brief interpretation of the text given by the two leaders. They raise the questions that the scripture suggested to them. What are one's obligations as a Christian? When is it right to witness by refusing to participate in a custom that reflects a different kind of belief? When is it disrespectful not to participate in such a custom; when might participating offer an opportunity to teach non-believers about Christ? If you are "puffed-up" in your knowledge of God, you risk behaving uncharitably, disrespectfully toward others.

It's sort of like having dinner with a vegan, one of the kids says in the discussion that ensues. You might like meat yourself, but you don't eat it out of respect for the person for whom vegetarianism is a moral imperative. Or like not drinking when you're around a recovering alcoholic. You don't drink as a means of showing your respect.

One of the adults tells about attending a Hindu wedding, at which the guests are expected to pledge respect to the Hindu god. Not to participate in the ritual would be an insult to the bridal couple, she knew; but she could not bring herself to make the pledge. Each situation is different, she says. All you can do is sit quietly and wait until you feel God pull you one way or the other.

Rules maintain a kind of forced respect, the group decides. They're rather like a traffic light. You stop or go based on what the light tells you. If everyone in the world knew God's grace, life would be more like a four-way stop, which causes people to stop for a moment, acknowledge the presence of others, and communicate with them to get through the intersection safely.

The leaders say a prayer; then there is silence while the group waits, heads bent. In quiet voices, one by one, individuals ask God to watch over their loved ones. They ask for strength, forgiveness. They give thanks for the gifts He has given. After each person speaks, the congregation murmurs, "Lord in your mercy, hear our prayer." In time, another silence falls. Then a hymn is sung, the offering taken in an upside-down tambourine, blessed.

When Communion is given, I find myself uncomfortable again, perhaps more so for one of the questions just considered. When is it disrespectful not to participate in a ritual in which you do not believe? Like the woman who spoke of the Hindu wedding, I heed my inner voice. To take communion would be false, it tells

59

me; so while the others file up to the altar, break off a piece of bread, drink from the bottle of grape juice, I remain, self-conscious, in my place.

But when I go to observe again, the next Sunday, John Lennon is singing "Imagine," and the leaders, a mother and daughter, ask the group to join in a circle so that we might celebrate Communion together. My inner voice says the same thing it said the week before: don't go; but to sit apart from the circle of worshipers, to risk in some way spoiling the ritual that is so obviously meaningful to every other person here seems inexcusably rude. So, I rise and go to the altar. I break off a tiny piece of bread, take a tiny sip of grape juice—as if to take such small portions could lessen my self-betrayal. I join the circle, all of us holding hands, swaying—no one, it seems to me, quite relaxed—to U-2's "Angel in Harlem."

I am relieved when it is over. Driving home, I finally see that, no matter how much I respect the faith of these students whom I love, my own feelings about Christianity, about group spiritual experiences in general, won't allow me to write about it objectively. The very questions I've been asking are faulty, unconsciously shaped by what I don't believe. This realization and a growing sense of my students' earnest hope for my salvation shocked me into learning again what I teach. Good writing is an act of self-discovery. The only questions that matter, writing about anything, are the ones we ask ourselves.

Every fall I take my band of teenage writers to Crown Hill Cemetery for an afternoon. It is a good place to visit because it is about dying, and anything about dying is about living as well. It is useful to wander among the graves of those whose lives are over. To feel grateful that you are still here, living the story of your life.

This year, the day we go is one of those last almost-warm days. The sky is cloudless, blue; the only leaves left on the trees are yellow. I spread a red-checked table cloth on James Whitcomb Riley's grave, put a tape of opera arias into the little boom box I've brought, and we eat our lunches. We talk about things we know and wish we knew. From where we sit, the skyline of the city we live in looks like Oz.

When we have finished, I send them off with their notebooks to explore and reflect. All but one girl, who has just finished writing a beautiful story about her mother, who died a few years ago, after a long illness, and who is buried here. I've brought flowers, and we take them to her mother's grave. Then we sit down on the grass and talk. She tells me about her mother: what she was like, how much she loved her and feared losing her. How empty she felt when she was finally gone. How, even now, she often cannot sleep at night.

She says, "The worst thing is, I wonder what my life would have been like if my mother hadn't died, and I can't even imagine it." As she speaks, I look up and see two deer standing among the gravestones in the distance. I touch her shoulder. "Look," I say. We sit quietly, and the deer begin to lope toward us. They come within twenty feet of where we sit, upon the grave. They are so beautiful, so graceful. Males with big antlers. They take a long look at us, then flick their white-bobbed tails, and bound away.

My student looks at me as if she's seen a ghost. "Maybe it's stupid," she says. "But do you think that meant something? A kind of sign?"

"Yes," I say. "Oh, yes."

And on this ordinary day, in this unlikely place, I am flooded with light. Again, teaching, I remember what I thought I knew: it matters to believe in Something. To be open to, deserving of the unexpected moments when it shows its vast, kind spirit.

60

THE FASHIONABLE CHURCH
Nancy Niblack Baxter

When a man arrived in the overgrown village of Indianapolis in the 1840s, the question as he disembarked from stagecoach or train was not, "How's he make a living?" Or even, "Is he married or spoken for?" It was, "How is he churched?" Historian Jacob Piatt Dunn described the rivalry which would go on, should the new arrival have no active affiliation. Would he grace the pews of the staid Presbyterians, the more emotional Methodists and Baptists, or the ever-communing Disciples of Christ? Presumably if "unchurched," he might visit them all on the Sundays to come, walking down the candlelit aisles on the arm of someone with a ruffle or two on her skirt to the stares of the "best families."

Going to church in Indianapolis has always been a social occasion, and almost as soon as they were built some churches achieved the status of being regarded as "fashionable." One of these was Christ Church on the Circle. It has remained fashionable to this day, and also effective as a church. But the height of the social factor in the lives of Indianapolis churches occurred in the 1890s, when magnificent structures replaced the simple frame buildings of the 1830s and '40s. The newly rich lieutenants of industry in the city and their ladies, to say nothing of their hoop-rolling kids, wanted to savor the scriptures in style.

Out of the gaslit mansions in such places as Irvington, Woodruff Place, and College Corners came churchgoers headed to Woodruff Place Baptist Church, First and Second Presbyterian, Roberts Park, and especially Meridian Street Methodist Church. The late Daniel Evans, in his book *At Home in Indiana for One Hundred Seventy-five Years, The History of Meridian Street United Methodist Church 1826-1996*, describes the squabbles over pew allocation, rivalry over who made the largest contribution, and focus on an architectural style which attempted to be "more elegant and chaste" than that of any other church in town. The scramble to demonstrate prestige and power through church building went on in a slightly different manner at the Indianapolis Hebrew Congregation, Beth El Zedek, and eventually Saints Peter and Paul Cathedral, which from 1905 to 1907 built the stately sanctuary which signified the coming of age of the northside Catholic community.

Fashionableness in churches—both on the part of individuals and on the part of the institution itself—had existed, of course, long before the 1890s. Going to church to see and be seen and to establish or reaffirm one's place in society is probably a part of human nature. But there's more to the subject than just the parade of fripperies on a Sunday morning with everybody watching. Indianapolis's so-called fashionable churches have been both the bane and the strength of our city's spiritual life.

I grew up in one of the most "fashionable" churches in Indianapolis, and so I know of what I speak. Central Avenue Methodist Church had been built around 1890, its plans designed to include five fireplaces, some with butternut mantels, a gorgeous panoply of gaslights to emblazon the ceilings, symbolic and expensive stained-glass windows, five kinds of wood at the altar, and the finest preacher congregational money could buy.

Its Sunday School, built in the next two decades, was considered impressive, and the facility included a real stage, gym, and a huge fellowship hall. All was prosperous, affirmative. To see the Sunday School picture taken in 1917 in front of the church doors, with more than a hundred people who would have also appeared in Indianapolis's Blue Book, is to observe a profusion of boas and furs, bowler hats and well fed faces reflecting satisfaction with having done their duty to remember the Sabbath Day.

What a glorious, interesting thing it was to attend a church where hundreds of healthy and attractive people crowded into the sanctuary to hear us recite on Children's Day, to watch the future leaders of the city and state dressed up for plays and pageants in the brightly lit "Globe Theatre" auditorium, or to listen to the "Central Avenue Orchestra" play at opening exercises for the Sunday School. There must have been twenty-five or thirty well scrubbed and halfway proficient young musicians in that group.

Today the church's written histories and the Historic Landmarks Foundation brochures emphasize that Central Avenue under noted minister Orien Fifer was a pioneer in the "Social Gospel" movement. I don't remember my parents and others who were there then talking about it that way. Good Christian things were happening surely, but in the thirties Central Avenue Methodist Episcopal Church seemed at heart to flower as a Mecca for wealthy and powerful families, now in their second generation of attending its services and missionary society and youth meetings. The talk after church was of hats, donations, and northside family divorces within the congregation. Perhaps thus has it ever been everywhere, but my memories are not of Social Gospel.

Certainly by the forties when I was a child attending Sunday School, though, Central Avenue's golden splendor had a tarnished edge. It was still a place where lots of somebodies with old Indianapolis names went. But no one of a different race or culture played in the gym; no black faces graced the chicken and noodle church suppers or raised their voices in the fellowship hall in a chorus of "The Happy Wanderer." And, as the eloquent ministers still made the mahogany rattle with their sermons, outside, the neighborhood at Twelfth and Central was slipping into poverty, decay, and despair. As a nine or ten-year-old I could see that. It puzzled me why we didn't seem to talk about why we were so "different" from everybody around us, though I did hear comments that "Kentucky people" had taken over the neighborhood.

Miss Butler, daughter of the university's founder, was a recluse in her Victorian home next to the church. As we walked to our autos we saw her walking warily about her yard, wearing a long black dress which brushed unmowed grass as high as a wheat field; Doberman pinschers sat near the wrought-iron fence protecting her. I sometimes thought the church was like her.

I went through Sunday School. The forties came to an end. The neighborhood around the church sagged into deeper disintegration. The drive from the North Side seemed longer; fewer of the congregation made it any more. Our Junior High Methodist Youth Fellowship caroled around the church one Christmas season about this time. After our raucous treatment of "Hark the Herald Angels Sing" a window opened on the second story of a two-story, rotting old mansion of the 1880s. It was a bunch of flats now; we trooped up the stairs; the door opened to a woman in an old house dress, radiantly smiling thanks for our performance. A "Kentucky woman."

I was the closest to her, so I mumbled, "We're from the church." My eyes roved behind her to the shabbiest of apartments; ragged linoleum could not conceal the holes in the floor. Clutter was everywhere; furniture scarce. A wretched cooking smell came from a one-burner stove in the corner of the room. A little boy of about four came forward, dancing a little to keep his feet off the cold floor. He looked up at us, staring at our pretty wool coats, bright Christmas pins on the girls' velvet collars. The expression in his eyes was full of awe and wonder at the world we represented, just one block away. I remember his bare little arm was out towards us; for some reason I wanted to touch his skin, which had soot marks on it. Probably it was eighth-grade curiosity more than anything else.

Down we trooped again, Capezio flats and Hush Puppies clacking on the steps. I don't believe I've ever been so unsettled in my life. The next year the "somebodies" whose names Indianapolis people would recognize decamped to 86th street, leaving those of us who didn't want to go staring at the holes (now covered) in the ceiling where the gaslights used to be. The decampers formed St. Luke's Methodist Church, soon to be one of the greatest Methodist congregations in the Midwest. My family joined another church, but what had happened to me, for wonderful and not-so-good at 12th and Central, stayed with me for the rest of my life.

Yet in a deeper way, for all the insensitivity to the needs of the poor and ethnically different, the emphasis on seeing and being seen, the surface spirituality, something happened at that church. It had to have happened inwardly to people. Even though Jesus did say it was difficult for a rich man to enter heaven, he didn't follow that with, "When two or three are gathered in my name they better not be prosperous." No. When I was nine years old, to the surprise of my parents, as the minister called for those who wanted to join the church to come forward, I went down the aisle and knelt on my knees at that altar. I've never gotten off them, figuratively speaking, ever since. So something was going on in that dimly lit fashionable church, I suspect for quite a few of us. The Gospel of Jesus is a very lively and life-altering message, and it can live amidst polished walnut and crystal as well as more humble places, though perhaps with more difficulty. A camel going through the eye of a needle has some trouble, especially when the "eye" is undergoing radical change. *63*

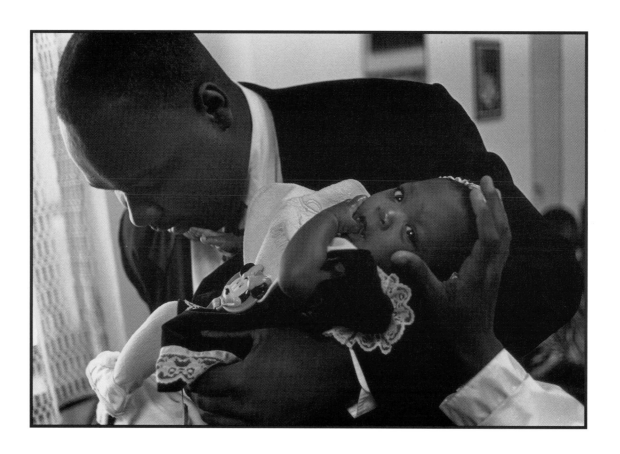

66

68

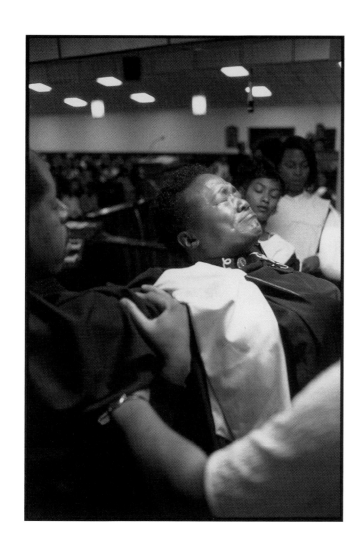

RECALLING: *A Theologian Remembers His Church*
Stephen H. Webb

My best friend growing up was a PK, the preacher's kid. I was merely the son of the chairman of the elders, and therein lies all the difference. Although through my eyes he possessed status and privilege that I had to earn, we both were born into a world that was all-encompassing, an eternal return of Sunday mornings saturating our every word and deed. More than just shaping our world, the church literally was our world, not only because of the time we spent there, twice on Sundays, Wednesday evenings, vacation Bible school, Saturday activities, but also due to the dinner table conversation, the gossip and the earnest talk about building funds and bus maintenance and attendance figures. The geography of my youth is populated with church talk and church people, and I still measure my world by what took place on 57 North Rural Street, at Englewood Christian Church, in Indianapolis, Indiana.

Andy, my friend, and I realized from the beginning that we had to conform ourselves to this place by becoming characters in its drama if we were to make it our own. We learned how to mythologize the church with our games, fears, and laughter. There were no boundaries, only our versions of a sacred grove or a magic stone: the yellow stairs, the boiler room, the dark hallway, rooms we were not supposed to enter and places we created on our own. Climbing to the top of the fire escape, we could imagine Moses on Mt. Sinai or Jesus being led by the devil to the pinnacle of the Temple, and the devil saying to him, "If you are the Son of God, throw yourself down!" We knew that the religious life was not possible without the power of temptation.

The people were also sacred and legendary, like the janitor who stole money and was caught with a special dye that only later made his hands turn purple, or the short, old man who would suddenly stand up during the service and quote scripture, and the quotes were somehow always appropriate, always well chosen. There was also the old man who had played semiprofessional baseball and who, after insisting that we shake hands, would squeeze so hard that I would lose my breath and hardly have time to cry. For several years on the way to church we would stop and pick up an elderly woman who claimed to be the granddaughter of the original "Little Orphant Annie," the servant girl who was made famous in the poem by James Whitcomb Riley.

We terrorized the Sunday School teachers, because we had no other way of saying who we were. As sons and heirs of authority, power, and grace, or so we felt, our arrogance must have made us unbearable. We both were sure that we heard the call to the ministry echoing through the church halls. We argued about which of us would someday preach behind the massive pulpit in the front and center of the sanctuary. When we inched down the dark hallway, which ran behind the sanctuary and up to the baptistery, we could hardly believe that the nervous laughter and strained voices were our own. We thought we owned the place, but of course, it owned us.

That church was the architecture of our spirituality, the shape, touch and feel of what we were supposed to become. It was a large building that had been expanded several times, so we never grew tired of exploring it. It was sacred because, in our young eyes, it was inexhaustible. By racing through its halls we were seeing if we could outrun it; by climbing onto its roofs we were seeing if we could ever even leave it behind. The irony is that by trying so hard to master it we ended up becoming such a part of it that we could never let it go.

The rhythmic punctuation of Sunday mornings was even then strange and dreamlike, and certainly now it is a world we can neither depart nor reclaim. Staying home on Sunday evenings to watch the Disney movie was, I imagined, the forbidden fruit of paradise, a joy forever beyond my reach. All of our fantasies and fears and dreams had to be channeled into the church, so that we knew no distinction between the sacred and the profane. Sunday morning was our Saturday night, and the worship service was our playground. We would roll the rubber rings that served as Communion cup holders down the sloping sanctuary floor toward the altar table, looking to see what faces would turn around, so that we would know whose feet they hit, and thus where they stopped. We would pass notes, play paper games, try to sneak the wallet from the purse of the woman in the pew ahead of us during one hymn and replace it during the next.

The building was functional, surrounded by old houses with no yards and a huge parking lot, an empty symbol of prosperity. The church was in the inner city, a step out of time, left behind in the flight to the suburbs. This was not a city on a hill but a neglected urban village. The people who ran it had once lived in that neighborhood, during better times, and now they had a reverse commute, driving for a half an hour back into the city to worship. Along with these suburban people, the church was full of the poor and the disadvantaged, the very people who kept appearing in the Gospel stories themselves. It did not take me long to realize that my friends at church were very different from my friends at school. I remember visiting a school friend's church in the suburbs and not being able to put my finger on it, but the all-white, well dressed,

confident and articulate congregation struck me as unreal, even as it made me question the reality of Englewood. That friend's church is the kind of church I go to today, educated, liberal and friendly, but for me all such churches lack a certain substance, as if they were novels with only one dimension, missing the strange characters who make a plot dramatic.

The church of my youth was part of the independent movement that had broken from the Disciples of Christ. Englewood was not really all that proud of this break; indeed, it did not think about the Disciples denomination (to which Andy and I now belong) much at all. Englewood traced a lineage directly from Barton Stone and Alexander Campbell to Richard A. Laue, my friend's father, our preacher. The independents do not recognize the claim of history, the contingency of all events and the ambiguity of all truths. The theology was restorationist, which meant that the earliest church, the stories of the Acts of the Apostles, were sufficient history for us. Dick Laue's charismatic sermons were one seamless whole of biblical proof texting, a dizzying collage of verses that all pointed to the single theme of salvation by grace alone, a message that had to be repeated continuously but which could be found in any and every Bible passage. The texture of the Bible was flattened into an interwoven textuality where every verse pointed to another verse and every word was transparent to the work of the cross.

The world was one, united by an eternal narrative that was simultaneously ancient and contemporary. There also was no need to deal with spatial connections, with worrying over other churches, church hierarchies, or the Christian world at large. The world was our world, and our world was this one church. The liberal problem of fitting the church into the modern world never arose, because this church denied the existence of any world other than the one it was. We stretched the biblical narrative to

71

make the plot for all of our stories, becoming characters in a drama that seemed to be written especially for us.

Englewood was never quite fundamentalist in today's sense of that term. The idea that the world needed Christianizing would have meant that the world needed recognizing, that there really were two worlds after all. Instead, there was talk about building up the body, contributing to the building fund, and buying more buses. To grow meant to absorb some of the surrounding world into our own, without surveying the boundaries that separated us. The buses would circle the poor neighborhoods surrounding the church, picking up children by offering prizes and thus boosting Sunday School numbers. Every Christmas these kids would be rewarded with apples and oranges. I never took any home, although I did help my father pass them out, feeling a bit ashamed to be giving away what I myself would not accept as a gift.

There is a picture hanging on a wall at my house of our church congregation taken in the parking lot by one of those cameras that rotates and thus could capture the entire half-circle of the over one thousand people who were in attendance that day. When I show friends this photograph, I cover up the date, because the thin black ties and wide lapels on the men and the stacked and layered hair on the women seem to come from the fifties rather than from 1970. I was not the only one who seemed totally oblivious to the Vietnam war, the counter culture, student protests and cultural revolutions. At age nine I am clutching a Bible, one knee on the pavement, exuding innocent sincerity. One year Dick Laue ran behind the crowd after the camera began rotating so that he could be on both ends of the picture, the alpha and omega of the church.

While we were very young, Andy and his family lived in the parsonage, which was located right next door to the church and at a glance indistinguishable from it. We spent every Sunday after-noon there. Sometimes we would go upstairs to his sister's room and play with her dolls. This ended one day when Andy's father came into the room and, in a clearly worried and startled voice, asked us what we were doing. "You boys shouldn't be playing with those. Why don't you get outside, do something fun." Eventually Andy's family too moved to the suburbs, so that our Sunday after-noons were spent at his house or mine, far removed from the church building. We would play pretend games, making up stories of cowboys or gangsters or detectives, but we hardly knew what world was real and what was mere make-believe. Playing and wor-ship were indistinguishable, a way of entering another world that was and was not our own.

Later, I got my own "dolls," a cowboy (Johnny West) and a sol-dier (a G.I. Joe), equipped with guns and bombs and camping gear. I had permission to let my imagination run wild, as long as it was encompassed not in the superfluous world of Barbies but in the world of suffering and violence. Just as we read the Gospels quickly in order to get to the great climax of the death of Jesus, pretend games were more acceptable if they involved the spilling of blood.

The Doctrine of the Atonement, how the death of Jesus saves us from sin, meant everything to us. After all, the New Testament exists to explain how a judicial murder can function as an event of unbounded love and mercy. We did not believe that Jesus was mere-ly a good teacher or a nice moral example. Something happened on the cross that was the equivalent to a cosmic earthquake, and in that bloody disaster we could find our own salvation. That Jesus died for us meant not that all violence is evil and grace is free but that all sins must be matched with suffering and grace is hard.

My father's temper was thus not out of step with the atone-ment that Dick Laue preached. The cross shows that justice demands punishment, that hardship is the necessary and appropri-

72

ate outcome of every transgression. My father came from a large family, most of whom remained in Kokomo when he ventured down to the big city of Indianapolis. His childhood had been difficult; his mom died when he was young and some of his older brothers ended up in hard times. Raising a family during the sixties and seventies reinforced his sense that order was a thin membrane of protection from chaos. I think he was always afraid that my brother and I would turn out to be no good, so he interpreted our independent and rebellious ways as signs that we were courting disaster. He believed in original sin, and he knew that we were not to be trusted. His only recourse was to try to break our wills with threats and punishments, hoping that we could be redeemed by violence. The heavenly Father, after all, saw no other way to save humanity than by sacrificing his very own son.

My parents worked together as a kind of atonement team: my mother suffered for us while my father made sure that we suffered to his satisfaction. My mother's job in the economy of our household was to be the giver, and for the most part her labor went unrewarded and even unremarked (just as her many years serving the church as its treasurer were never taken seriously by the men who made the decisions in the church). Her sacrifices seemed inevitable and natural, as necessary as the passion of Jesus, although I do not think she thought of her deeds as heroic or dramatic. My mother vicariously labored on our behalf, while my father methodically enforced his rigid standards of behavior, believing that nothing less than retribution could satisfy any breaking of the law. Between the two of them was a Calvinist Christology in the making. Forgiveness was not enough; there had to be some pain, some objective evidence of the wages of sin in order to restore the balance and harmony of our relationship. It was a tragic worldview that I now see to be irreconcilable with the comedic nature of the Gospels, the way in which

Jesus sets everyone free from all guilt through outrageous acts of love and mercy. It was also a worldview that made me value even more the intense combination of freedom and submission that Andy and I experienced in church.

Like the God they preached and worshipped, the world of Englewood tried not to change. There was a brief Pentecostal movement but Englewood was not ready for tongue-speaking and prophecies, so the charismatics left. There was also an argument over baptism, whether it was absolutely necessary for salvation, and the faction, led by my dad and Andy's, who took the view that it was not, stayed, but only after a long battle and heavy attrition. Finally, there was an argument over the power of the minister and his relationship to the elders. Dick thought that the preacher was set apart from and in charge of the elders, rather than being just one elder among many. Although the preacher won this battle, with my dad's reluctant support, it took its toll, and he left. Andy left when he was thirteen and I was fourteen, and I guess that going to church has never been the same for me since.

We were twins, not least because, when very young, our mothers dressed us alike, my mom making two of everything. Somehow, though, I never felt like the church was really mine, as much as it served as a second house, a home to our first house. Andy, with his golden hair and self-assured ways, was the favored son. He seemed to define gracefulness for me, and people then, as now, gravitate to his effortless exercise of generosity, the way in which he exudes the energy of life. Although I was older by one year, I was younger, in a way. I always thought that Andy, as the PK, had the first place at the altar, that he was the real heir. I had to try harder to receive the same attention, and often I felt like Cain to his Abel, that somehow my offerings were not as acceptable. My struggle to claim the blessing that he possessed at his

73

very core made me more cunning and questioning, and thus my vocation of theology was born out of a great ambivalence. I am obsessed with thinking about Christianity, but I never know if I am trying to free myself from it or free myself for it.

There was always tension between us, probably more on my part than his. The Bible is full of sibling rivalry, brothers battling for a birthright. Early Christian theologians were quick to pick up on the idea that the younger brother usually wins these conflicts. The younger brother is chosen in spite of the illegitimacy of his claim, thus showing the sheer gratuity of grace. Was I Esau to Andy's Jacob? The most famous New Testament story of brothers is the prodigal son, who left behind his older brother, still toiling, resentfully, in the fields. Was I the all-too-reasonable older brother, or were we both prodigal sons? Did we ever really leave, and could we ever return home?

Many years later Andy and I lived in the same small town in Indiana for several years, where I was trying to get tenure at Wabash College and Andy's partner was there on a visiting appointment. Wabash has the feel of a world set apart, where all of the energy is directed inward, not outward. The faculty focus is on the students, and the students themselves play hard at their work and work hard at their play. The small and intense setting of the college allowed Andy and me to share an allegorical space. The people we met always reminded us of someone from Englewood, and the arguments we had reduplicated the fights of our childhood. It seemed to us that we had found Englewood all over again. Now when we talk about Wabash College we realize that, as with everything else, we are really recalling Englewood, which is our own eternal shibboleth, a password to the past. Englewood is the root metaphor for our lives, and we cannot outgrow it.

Wabash College is a powerful place because, in its relation to Englewood, it is an alternative world, like something out of a science fiction novel, a world that doubles reality, like religion itself. What we shared during our years at Wabash was not something repetitive and derivative, but a wonderful return of our friendship, as if what we were was something that could eternally come to be again and again. What we shared was not just who we once were, but the ways we were trying both to be and not to be the past again. We were internal exiles, unsure if we were looking for a way home or if we had never really left.

I had been at Wabash for several years when Andy and his partner (who, like me, is an alumnus of the College) arrived. They brought a new energy to the place, just when I was trying my best to conserve my own energy. They spent freely like prodigal sons who have returned home unchanged. They wanted both to be at home and to spend like tourists, in effect making the entire campus their home. The result was that Andy somehow seemed more at home at Wabash than I did, even though he was there temporarily, and I had a continuing position on the faculty. What Andy and his partner brought to Wabash was a decision, which constituted their every gesture, that their premise of action was a desire to be there and only there. They seemed to be everywhere on campus, but they were active in graceful and fluid ways, in contrast to the frustrated and frantic energy of the overworked faculty. They practiced a kind of squandering, a dissemination of meaning that broke barriers and transgressed boundaries, a lavishing that showed, by contrast if nothing else, that the College's ordinary economy of relentless and rushed expenditures is in the end frugal and timid and void of any real purchasing power. They practiced a shadow economy, a black market, a kind of supply-side economics that showed that all you have to do is spend, and all good things will return to you. We at

Wabash had forgotten, I think, how to spend, how to waste, how to live in luxury. We had become, really, all too reasonable, serious, careful, cautious, and prudent.

My own economy, to use that language, was more careful and circumspect than Andy's. I had become a bit sullen, letting my responsibilities overwhelm me, running around in a state of hyper-activity. I was constantly thinking about whether I wanted to be elsewhere, while Andy and his partner, like good mystics, actually enjoyed each moment as it came, without begrudging it. My busy-ness was a kind of religious fever, a false way of gaining transcen-dence from my situation by a constant activity of diversion. After a period of this hustling diligence, I found myself wanting to pro-tect my time and my space from all of the demands being put upon me. In order to pursue my own work, I withdrew a bit from the College and then found that I no longer knew how to give to the College in spontaneous and generous ways. Indeed, there is some-thing in me that shrinks from giving too much to people, from becoming entangled in gift giving, and I think that comes from my sensitivity (at times an allergy) to the responsibilities and obliga-tions that giving creates. I am the son, after all, of an elder, an organizer and worrier, not the preacher, the charismatic leader. I am the older, unprodigal brother, all too rational and circumspect, and yet I too want to find my way by crossing boundaries and transgressing the rules that maintain order.

I often find myself wondering what I am trying to do in the classroom, whether I am recreating Englewood or trying to exorcise its hold on me. My position as a professor of religion allows me to offer the kind of religious education that I never had but sometimes wish I had had, full of sophisticated questions and historical depth, a passionate and committed questioning of the Christian heritage. With my authority as a theologian I can take the place of the fig-ures of my youth who still hold me with such great power that I do not want to let them go. My classroom is my church, where I can be both outlandish and serious, a spiritual guide and a provocateur. By being a religious teacher I can also challenge the conventions and presuppositions of my colleagues, who do not think that reli-gion should play any constructive role in the academy. Andy also found a way to remain true to his calling while journeying beyond Englewood, that is, to be a preacher outside the church. He became a social worker and therapist, and people were naturally attracted to his charismatic and healing manner.

After a few years at Wabash, Andy's partner got another job, out west, and it was another ending. I was the older broth-er who ended up with the inheritance after all. I knew that this new break in our lives would not have the same impact because we had already been broken, had already left each other so long ago. When we were boys and his family was moving to a new church, in California, we argued, and he threw my jacket in a creek near his house, and I was too stubborn to retrieve it. It was a cold and windy day, and neither of us would venture into the creek to save what was left of our world. We were dramatizing our forced separation, trying to make the decisions of the adult world our own. We were falling out of innocence, yet sometimes I wonder how far we have really come.

Once during those Wabash years we returned to Englewood for a Sunday service. Englewood had changed as much as my father had. My dad not only became much more mellow with the passing of the years, but he also helped orga-nize a homeless shelter for women and children in the aban-doned school building next to the church. Now that we are both older, we are closer than ever before. When I visit Englewood, I am forced to realize that my father probably has changed over

75

the years more than I have, and that he and some of his Englewood friends are actually doing the slow, hard work for the poor that I often only talk about.

During this visit, however, Andy and I were not interested in the present. We were there to see how far we could sneak back into our past. After everyone else had left the building, we went up the yellow stairs and down the dark hallway. Stepping softly, as if we were trying to hear something, we found the door to the baptistery and entered the long and narrow pool, which hangs suspended like a balcony above the sanctuary. There we stripped our clothes for a brief immersion into the bitterly cold water of our past. I jumped out as quickly as I jumped in, but Andy stayed and splashed, part drowning and part swimming, and we both laughed, like King David dancing before the ark. I could not tell if what we were doing was sacred or profane. Clearly, the transgressions of our youth, just as the transgressions of our present, were the stuff that made church

seem real to us. Only by crossing the social and moral boundaries within the church, its customs and rules and regulations, did we feel free and in touch with the mystery that had such a hold on us. Only by being prodigal could we feel at home, yet our prodigality condemned us to always feel homeless. We had to make ourselves outsiders from within in order to experience the transcendence that makes spirituality possible.

The last time we were together, we talked about grace. What would it mean, one of us suddenly blurted out, if God's love really were unconditional? What would it be like to live a grace that is abundant and free? The world really would be one large Englewood, full of legends and magic, one huge sacred grove for play and worship. Every day would be both a Sunday morning and the weekend, a true Sabbath of piety and mischievous pleasure, the sacred made possible by the profane.

BIRTHDAY POEM

Etheridge Knight
INDIANAPOLIS, INDIANA, 1975

The sun rose today, and
The sun went down
Over the trees beyond the river;
No crashing thunder
Nor jagged lightning
Flashed my forty-four years across
The heavens. I am here.
I am alone. With the Indianapolis/News

Sitting, under this indiana sky
I lean against a gravestone and feel
The warm wine on my tongue.
My eyes move along the corridors
Of the stars, searching
For a sign, for a certainty

As definite as the cold concrete
Pressing against my back.
Still the stars mock
Me and the moon is my judge.

But only the moon.

'Cause I ain't screwed no thumbs
Nor dropped no bombs—
Tho my name is naughty to the ears of some
And I ain't revealed the secrets of my brothers
Tho my balls've / been pinched
And my back's / been / scarred—

And I ain't never stopped loving no / one
O I never stopped loving no / one

THE DESERT OF EDEN
Jim Poyser

I am bundling up my blonde-haired boys. Sweaters, sweatshirts, heavy coats, boots. I stuff their hands into mittens, place stocking hats on their heads. It's the dead of winter and we're off to the Indianapolis Zoo.

My boys, aged four and six years old, think I'm nuts. There's no end to their complaints, no shortage of outrage, but I persist. The winter is the only time I can truly tolerate the zoo, take in its awful spectacle, the beauty and sadness of the caged animal.

A winter visit to the zoo requires special conditions: the colder the better; the deeper the snow the more desirable. Weekends? Forget it. The middle of the week is ideal. Last night, with six or so inches of snow already on the ground, it began to rain, creating a nice slick plane of ice on the streets. Then more snow fell, making a deceptive carpet over the ice.

Today, the temperature is in the low teens, making the wind-chill plummet into the subzero range. Snow flurries fall, are caught by the wind and sculpted into momentary tornadoes. The brilliant sun catches certain snowflakes precisely, making them flare like a flashbulb. The color of the cloudless sky is the blue that gave birth to all hues of blue.

Cold, ice, snow, drifts, swirls, sunlight, a Thursday. A perfect day to go to the zoo, despite my sons' protestations. Today, I can guarantee: we will be the only customers at the zoo. The animals will outnumber the humans.

I have a fantasy when these events conspire. I imagine that it's the end of the world, and we're at the zoo. All of civilization has been destroyed save for this Ark of a zoo. My sons and I inspect the remains of our world, moving silently through this cathedral of nature. The possibility that my two sons and I could, along with these scant species of animals, somehow manage to repopulate the earth, is of course as ridiculous as a literal interpretation of the myth of Noah's Ark. Even if we brought along my wife, we still couldn't start the human species all over again.

My boys are dressed, wrapped in their winter-wear, leaning against the front door, hoping I won't actually make them get into the car. I open the door and the cold air smacks us in the face. Eight inches of snow rests upon the ground. Yes. A fine day. An end-of-the-world kind of day.

We get in the car and after some cranking of the engine, it actually starts. To the zoo we go.

"Everywhere animals disappear," writes John Berger. "In zoos they constitute the living monument to their own disappearance." It's estimated that 125 million Americans visit the country's zoological parks. This number represents more people than attend all professional football, baseball, and basketball games combined.

It seems that urban societies, having lost touch with the instinctual world, need the zoo to connect them to their ancestral past. The naturalist E. O. Wilson would call this connection biophilia: "the innately emotional affiliation of human beings to other living organisms."

In all cultures, throughout time, animals have had immeasurable impact—not only in the labor of that culture, but on its creativity and spiritual systems. Animals have acted as agents to the gods, as well as being revered as deities themselves. Classical antiquity, for example, believed the bear to be a symbol of creation. Myths of the spirituality of animals abound, from the cat cult of ancient Egypt, to the messenger fox of the Japanese rice god Inari, to the monkey god Hanuman in Hinduism.

We need look no further than the astrological systems to see how animals lord over the earth. In the Western astrological system, eight of the twelve constellations represent animals. In the Chinese zodiac, all twelve constellations are animals.

This is no small matter. There was a time when the study of the heavens was the main driving force of culture. Astrology combined religion, art and science in one endeavor—and animals played (and play) an integral role.

I try to inculcate my boys with respect, fear, and love of animals, but they get so many mixed messages from their culture. Animals are used for every purpose, from food to clothing to entertainment.

As we drive to the zoo, these and other thoughts assail me. It's been a long, downhill ride for the poor beasts. After millennia of fear and worship, humans began to domesticate animals. Fossil findings indicate that dogs, for example, have been domesticated since at least 9600 B.C. Animal husbandry turned animals not only into a tool for farming, but the farm itself.

The caging of wild animals has been practiced for thousands of years. The zoo goes back at least as far as the royal menageries of ancient Greece, Rome, and Mesopotamia. Exotic animals served as appropriate gifts for rulers of one land to present to another. Gifts, objects of wonder, symbols of human might, animals have long suffered the jingoistic tendencies of humanity. As Berger puts it, zoos were "an endorsement of modern colonial power."

In a way, this domination of animals reached its peak—or its pit—in the age of Descartes, who visualized beasts as mere machines. Descartes likened the makeup of animals as "a clock, which is made up merely of springs and wheels..."

Increasingly, the placing of animals in captivity has served a purpose beyond entertainment. The human sprawl has eliminated land and water environs, forcing animals into smaller and smaller areas. Pollution, poaching, and overpopulation have combined to cause an extraordinary extinction rate. And so zoos have found themselves charged with a mission to, in the words of Stephen Kellert, "provide genetic reservoirs for endangered species."

Zoos, then, have become a zootopia, a haven from the flood of civilization. We now know that a broad genetic pool is essential for species survival. Incest among humans is a moral taboo in part because it's a genetic disaster. Animals need a wide range of DNA to mingle with—or the results are extinction.

The Indianapolis zoo, in fact, trafficks in this DNA crapshoot on a prestigious level. Because the Indy zoo harbors the most important, from a genetic standpoint, snow tiger in North America. Her name is Lena.

Writer Stephen Kellert says zoos are "but a shallow reflection of wild reality, and the confinement of innocent creatures for human amusement may exert a degrading effect." Zoos, in fact, can "actually bolster the illusion of human hegemony, leaving the average visitor more arrogant than ever."

As we approach the entrance of the Indy zoo, the lady in the zoo-booth doesn't hide her amazement. She didn't expect any visitors today. She takes our zoo pass, smiling. A prominent sign warns: Some Animals May Not Be On Display.

79

If my theory holds, the animals not on display will most certainly include the human animal. I unfold the double stroller and my boys climb in; they sit like royalty as we begin moving.

Every zoo has its narrative structure. I like the Indy zoo because it places the fish house at the beginning. Life first began in the sea before moving on land. It only seems appropriate to begin a zoo with marine life. Other zoos, such as the Madison, Wisconsin, zoo, display their monkey house first.

We delay entering the warmth of the fish house and move to the sea lions. We approach quietly, spotting five or six sea lions resting peacefully in the water. They barely even bob, and we remain quiet, mesmerized by the sight.

The sea lions are usually the friskiest captives of the zoo. I've never seen them so taciturn. One sea lion is facing us, eyes closed, the only movement the contraction and expansion of his nostrils. Finally, he opens his eyes and spots us; a moment later he disappears into the water. This sets up a chain reaction—the others quickly submerge, too, then the entire group begins swimming energetically. We know we can see this better from the inside that looks into their waters and so we move into the fish house itself, welcoming its warmth.

We slowly pass through the first part of the fish house, noting the diversity of colors—and facial expressions. Next in the building is the jungle area, with its alligators and fish, and thirty-foot-long anaconda.

We ponder the snake's great length as we shed a few layers—it's hot and humid in the jungle, and we've come from the arctic hinterlands. It's actually a shock to see the anaconda out in full, protracted display. I've never seen him before—he's usually hidden. Perhaps the sign at the entrance to the zoo should have contained a footnote: Some Animals Who Otherwise Hide May Display Themselves Today.

I'm figuring that the lack of audience has made the anaconda bold, but as I quiz a passing zoo employee my hypothesis is dashed. Paul is his name, and with his beard and general rugged, outdoorsman demeanor, he seems profoundly content in his job. He tells me the behavior of the animals is more based on the weather conditions than the human crowds. The temperature of the air is much more a factor than scrutiny. He has no explanation, then, for why the anaconda is so forthcoming today. It's not as if the snake's atmospheric surroundings ever change.

His remarks make me think about the enormity of the support system necessary to provide a slice of ecosystem for each animal. Habitats are not easily thrown together. The more exotic the animal, the more complex the support system.

We move on, then, coming to the massive window that shows us the sea lions' playscape. Activity is quiet as we approach; perhaps they're quietly bobbing on the surface again. One small sea lion, however, is drifting like a dirigible around and around the space. I recognize her and hold my finger to the glass.

As she approaches, I move it down, then around, and she responds—as she has many times before—by curling around, following my finger as I trace it along the glass. My boys move to the window, extending their fingers like conductors awaiting the first moment of a symphony.

Before long, the entire community of sea lions—six or seven of them—is dancing with our fingers, flying past, somersaulting and spinning in synchronization like crazy state fair rides. We splendor in their mischief and grace for a long time. To contemplate these highly-evolved beings is one of the zoo's greatest pleasures, but it's time to move on. It's not easy to go; the next stop is the polar bears, and I'd rather avoid their neurotic pacing.

Fortunately, they are quiet today. Other days, these great

80

beasts pace back and forth in a kind of despair—I fear for their state of mind; are they bi-polar polar bears? Today, however, they appear peaceful, and the boys marvel at their thick coats of fur, enormous paws, and the great gusts of breath they expire. I begin the toil of mummifying my sons in their winterwear again.

The outdoors awaits us. The stinging temperature and the slippery slopes. And Lena, she's out there, too. Lena is the number one Amur tiger in all of North America. The Species Survival Program (SSP) says so, and it's their business to know. The SSP keeps a kind of genealogical map, a "dating service" as they call it, that lists the genetic relationship between the tigers throughout the continent. Lena is the most important, because she's come from the wilds of Siberia. The majority of snow tigers in captivity were born in captivity.

She and her brother were brought to the U.S. some four years ago. They were found, as cubs, after poachers had killed their mother. Lena's capture made the pages of *National Geographic*, and she's been no stranger to publicity since. Most recently, a Peter Mathiesson essay in *The New Yorker* retold her story. She's rich in exotic DNA. And she's a female. That makes her a special vessel in North America, nigh near a goddess.

The boys and I move quickly to the Forests section of the zoo, hoping to catch a glimpse of Lena. We are disappointed, however. She's not on "display," nor is the snow tiger imported from the Minneapolis Zoo anywhere in sight. I have mixed feelings about this. I wanted to see the great beasts, but I respect their privacy.

If all goes well, Lena will soon be pregnant, and the genetic pool of North American snow tigers will have been greatly enriched. If she does give birth, it's a success story for the zoo-as-Noah's-Ark enthusiasts. Despite the flood of poachers and civilization, the zoo contains a haven for reproductivity, for a chance at species survival.

It's important to keep in motion over the next part of our trek. This is the long haul as we finish with the Forests exhibit and move on to the Plains. The elephants present a puzzle. How adaptable can an animal be, after all? The African elephant making the adjustment to living in Indiana?

We observe a mealtime moment among the elephants. Four beasts are spread out as a zoo employee brings a bale of hay outside. Two elephants saunter over to the zoo worker as he cuts the bale and kicks the hay around to break it into bits. The two elephants wait, gently swinging their trunks. Their two comrades slowly approach, and it's only when all four are gathered that they begin to eat the hay. Now that's manners, I point out to my sometimes barbaric boys. They wrinkle their noses at me from beneath their stocking caps.

I feel like an intruder at the lions display. The sign proclaims that two cubs were born a few months prior. I spy them; they're beautiful cubs. Yet I suddenly realize: they've never known wilderness. All they've known is this zoo life. I wonder: do they dream of the wild?

The big surprise of the day thus far is the emu. Before today, I have passed by these creatures rather quickly. After all, they are at the end of the Plains, and especially when I've got my sons with me, I'm more than ready to complete this part of the trip. Something about the emu, however, nags at me, so I push the boys up to the fence and wait.

One approaches tentatively. Emus are large, three-toed birds. Long-necked, covered in feathers, it struts with a deliberate gait. It approaches, then boldly sticks its head over the fence, aiming for me. I realize, suddenly, that my winter jacket is brown—the same color brown that Paul and the other zoo folks wear.

This gives us the opportunity to view this strange beast up close. And more than any other animal on view today, it begs the

81

86

88

THE EMPTY GARDEN Hooverwood, March 1997
Alice Friman

In the Myth of the Garden
was the beginning.
The pulse
that pulls us all life long

back to the fountain,
the apple trees, the beds
of wild silence.
What difference the day?

Sabbath crowns *every* morning,
eases the shades at night.
But there *is* no return.
I wish I could tell you

different: how in this
nursing home, the oldest
of old who've lived so long
and are so close

are pulled to this garden
where they wait, huddled
in afghans,
clutching teddy or doll

and tip their faces to the sun.
Or sit by a window
taking delight
in the progress of spring,

schooling themselves on bulbs—
their green tongues, the pink
or yellow kiss
of a one-shot flower.

Or this: how each dawn
before the nurses unlatch
and lower the bed rails, an army
of the bent and trembling,

the arthritic, the feeble
and forgetful, rise
like crumples of paper
from their beds—your mother

and mine—stooped
and tottering histories
in slippersocks and flannel,
and hanging on furniture

work a path to the window
for that first cold blade of light
that's hacked its way
through blinds to find them.

If only, if only.
Then I too could believe
in an almost-angel mother
knocking on windowglass

to her friend, the only
face she recognizes—
the other cloudy wonder
across the courtyard—and she

waving back, nodding *yes yes*
and pointing
this daffodil or that
as if this day at least

she understood, clap
your hands and sing. Spring
is back and waiting for us
in the garden. Sassy

and hopeful
as a yellow school bus opening
and closing its wheezy door
then out the gates at last.

89

PILGRIMAGE ON THE FLAT LAND
Sandy Eisenberg Sasso

There is a time for birth and a time for loss and nowhere is that better known than in the body of a woman. The flow of life mirrored in the changing of the seasons knows that it cannot always be summer, that corn turns to seed, green stalks dry brown, that rain and sun come of their own accord, regardless of human desire.

We are accustomed to revelations born atop some mountain. It is to the high places we make our pilgrimages. But the rich Indiana soil boasts no glorious peaks poking into the ethereal heavens. Viewing Indianapolis from an airplane is like opening one of those popup children's picture books. On an otherwise monotonously flat surface, a three-dimensional scene suddenly unfolds. So it is that the center of the city juts out of a flat plain that extends for miles.

When I first decided to come to Indianapolis in 1977 to join my husband in leading a congregation, I could not imagine what midwestern wasteland awaited me. An Easterner by birth and education, I wondered how a Jewish community could possibly thrive in the Bible belt. If being Jewish would make me an oddity in the landscape of church steeples, then being a woman rabbi in a flatland of religious conservatism would brand me bizarre. I envisioned myself standing alone in a city of white bread and sweet corn, when my soul yearned for thick crusted rye and sweet rugelach. I did not expect this less than dramatic midwestern landscape to be a place where woman's spirituality could take root, where I might find a community of like-minded pilgrims. Yet Indiana has been home to some of the first women to be ordained as Episcopal priests, women rab-

bis, and a woman cantor. On the north side of the city, half of Christian Theological Seminary graduates are women. In 1997 a woman was elected Episcopal Bishop of Indianapolis.

My religious studies have been a guide on many a pilgrimage. The journey has led me to some lofty heights walking with Abraham up to Mt. Moriah and with Moses to the top of Sinai. It has carried me with Elijah ascending Mt. Carmel. There were steep climbs and dizzy descents.

But mountains and ladders with angels coming up and going down did not find a resting place in my newly acquired Indiana home. What spirit takes root in the flat land which sprouts white sugar corn, sweet orange persimmons, and cool urban limestone?

Perhaps women's spirituality finds itself at home in a landscape whose beauty is discovered in small things and where the holy must reveal itself on level ground. I decided to sit with women, as I had so long climbed with Abraham, Moses, and Elijah, and to listen to their stories.

When Hoosier women talk of spirituality, they speak of the theology of the thorn bush, of small revelations. Revelations sprout hope like crocuses in winter and hang like billowing white sheets on an ordinary clothesline in the spring. They are woven into the lace and linen delicately preserved from the old country. For Shermie Schafer, a Unitarian minister and hospice counselor, her carefully chosen home becomes a window to the sacred that may be nothing more or nothing less than three thirty-year-old blue spruces she names the three sisters. Cathy Cox, the director of an interreligious human rights coalition, said, "I first became aware of the presence of God sitting under a willow tree. I thought this couldn't be a mistake." For Marianne Towne, president of Church Women United, "The place where I go for spiritual renewal is my backyard."

In the Midwest, the soul is nourished not just on the wooden pews of church and synagogue but in the rich moist soil of the garden. The movements of the spirit are not only prayer and ritual but hauling and raking, digging and planting. "God's house is out in what God has made," Gwen Yeaman says of the earth's holiness.

Gwen introduces me to the culture of the Woodland People who, by their own account, have made Indiana their home for over 12,000 years. She refers to herself as a "tradition bearer" and weaves a story of the spirit which she is reluctant to put into words.

A Woodland house, whenever possible, opens to the east where the sun rises and the rhythms of the earth beat in the human heart. As life constantly recreates itself in the patterns of the seasons, in birth, death, and rebirth, women sense a connection to their own physical life cycles. The Divine is less an Absolute from on high to be grasped and obeyed, than a process to be experienced and celebrated on earth.

Gwen Yeaman hands me a sachet of tobacco. She tells me about the tradition of spreading the tobacco over a body of water or holding it up to the wind so that your prayers will be carried to the Creator. I am reluctant to let go of this remembrance of our meeting, but I *will* let it go, knowing that this meeting, like so many invisible gifts of the spirit, will remain with me.

It is not only from the soil that women harvest their spiritual metaphors, but from asphalt and concrete. We touch the sacred within the heart of metropolis.

Katherine Tyler Scott, director of Trustee Leadership Development, speaks of Monument Circle, this place of gather-

ing, as holy. But it is not the limestone Soldier's and Sailor's Monument that rises 284 feet above the Indianapolis center that evokes awe, but the circle at its base, embraced by Christ Church Cathedral and the Indianapolis Symphony Orchestra, the script of the soul written in music and fellowship. It is a space where people congregate on a warm Indiana afternoon to talk, to munch on a brown-bag lunch. Here ethnic festivals play new rhythms and offer the smells and sights of other countries and cultures. Wherever there is community, Hoosier women see a window to the spirit. If the traditional religious pilgrimage can be characterized as an ascent, then women's sacred dance may be choreographed as this embrace.

Midwestern spirituality, suggests Marti Steussy, a seminary Bible professor, abhors waste. "Waste is an awful thing—waste of time, of people, of things. You don't just discard, you treasure what you have."

When women hold as precious every act, they witness grandeur in small gestures of economy and domesticity. Even in the everyday task of feeding a child, the spirit rises like yeast left to rest in a warm kitchen. "Our son discovers peas," writes Bonnie Maurer, poet and teacher.

. . .

God of small and few teeth.
God of peas.
How can I explain my joy
gathering the collided planets
he has thrown to the floor,
how he peers at me
from his high chair...
for what galaxy he has made.

Bonnie counts sacred moments from the bits and pieces of chrome and spidered glass gathered from her father's junkyard, the pond full of algae before which her mother sat to paint, and links the apparently insignificant with the cosmic. If spirituality finds itself in the stewardship of small things, it expresses itself in the dynamic of the interpersonal. Between one and another, the soul is nourished.

Having traditionally been denied a voice in the public square, women often experience the spirit as it moves through interior space. "In the space I exist, the body of woman," says Ann Jones, teacher, activist, and wife of the former Episcopal Bishop of Indianapolis; "I identify with women who are barely surviving, those on the bottom of the ladder." Having been on the margins economically, politically, religiously, women understand what it means to be disenfranchised; they know the heart of the stranger.

When Indiana women speak of spirituality, the city both blesses and disturbs the pastoral soul they still carry within them. The blessing of the city is its diversity—color, accent, flavor. Churches, synagogues, mosques, Bahai Temple, and Hindu community center tell a story of religious pluralism that would surprise anyone who remembers this as a place where the Ku Klux Klan once flourished. If you listen closely, you can hear Spanish and Russian intermingled with midwestern twang. To the women who bring their rural childhood home into a growing metropolis, the varieties of culture and faith are among the city's greatest assets. Feminism, if it is true to itself, is by nature inclusive.

Indianapolis is not a homogeneous city, but there are places where you can still believe that fiction. You can lose yourself in the open spaces and live as if everyone is just like you. You need to claim your particular identity or else risk for-

feiting it. "Coming to Indianapolis was important in whatever closeness I have to Judaism," reflects Sharon Mishkin. "Here I have to choose to be Jewish."

If the blessing of Hoosier hospitality serves up fried biscuits and apple butter, the dark side of midwestern insularity remains suspicious of the outsider. Home-grown Indiana civility dictates that we do not act impulsively; it also means that we do not always acknowledge the tensions bubbling beneath the surface of city life. Katherine Tyler Scott speaks of the two faces of ignorance. It can open its doors to a few of anything. It marvels at the mysterious. But when the quaint becomes ordinary and demanding, ignorance slides into intolerance.

Linda Ferreira, a psychologist and instructor of gender issues in therapy, talks about the city's extremes which range from genuine graciousness to ugly rejectionism. "Where a life splits apart so freely," she asks, "how do I bridge the gap and not just line up on one side or another? How do I challenge intimidation and offer a way for accessible confession?" The polarities that fray the warp and woof of city life require a center where encounter can weave threads of healing.

No matter how many locks we place on our doors to try to prevent it, city lights and shadows seep through crevices and moldings. Urban life does not politely wipe its feet on doormats before entering. Women hint at the possibility of letting home creep out into the city, of bringing the hearth into the heart of municipal life, of doing some urban homemaking.

There is always the possibility of creating space to be more human, to make a place, a neighborhood, a city the ground where you can experience the grace of God. Whether minister, nun or laity, Jewish, Christian, or Muslim, women speak of structuring space for hospitality, rather than functionality. Rearranging rows of chairs into circles, women design places for gathering and creativity.

Harriet Clare opened a feminist bookstore in 1982. She deliberately chose a one-story residence to house Dreams & Swords. It was more than a locale to buy good literature; it was where women came to meet and talk, to feel safe, at home. It's the spaces in between the booklined walls, adorned with conversation and the stories of people's lives, that filled the spirit of the place.

The marketplace buys and sells bricks and mortar to erect structures. Women create space where the value of home seeks to build communities.

"Indianapolis is small enough to make it possible to find community. Spirituality grows here beyond the walls," observes Mary Gaul, a psychotherapist and member of Willowind Coven. She is part of the Wiccan tradition, which honors the goddess and seeks the sacred in all things. She speaks of life's interconnectedness and underscores one of her group's guiding principles–to do no harm. Seasonal rituals are celebrated in each other's homes, space made sacred by a gathering of sisters.

Freshly baked bread on a kitchen table opens another window to the holy. For Ann Jones, "Bread is a reminder that everyday God appears, but we often don't think about how it gets to us. When we pay attention, we remember to say a prayer and be grateful."

Gratitude, appreciation, wonder are spirituality's handmaidens. The sacred shouldn't have to shout to be noticed. Haughty holiness is an oxymoron. The ego's hubris is refined in the humility of the soul.

But women's spirituality is tied up, as well, with a certain bravado. After all, for centuries what women thought, felt, and said about the sacred has not come down to us. When seeking an image for their soul-struggle, they heard Abraham listening to angels from God and found themselves eavesdropping with Sarah outside the tent. For women to act not just as descen-

dants, eavesdroppers on a holy tradition, but as ancestors, creators along the spiritual journey, is audacious behavior. Women are making themselves a seat at tradition's table, pouring their woman soul into Scripture, prayer, and ritual.

When Reverend Anne Byfield, minister of Robinson Community AME Church first became a pastor, she was apologetic about being a woman so as not to offend anyone. She tried to be neither male nor female and then heard God say, "I called you because you are a woman. You bring the pain and healing of your life." Reverend Byfield views her ministry as offering the wounds and strengths of society as gifts to God. "They come back home in a way that leaves me strong without tearing apart who I am."

Susan Bettis, a feminist scholar and lecturer on women's spirituality, honors the variety of traditions that take root here and adds her own distinctively female voice. She brings together the diverse touchstones of those faiths and weaves the Divine feminine voice into newly fashioned seasonal rituals. Hoosier-grown women's spirituality does not easily discard the sacred forms of traditional religions. It holds them gently and, with courage, blows a woman's breath through their hallowed vessels.

How does the transcendent move through the body and soul of a woman? Sister Jean Alice sees in women bonding together and sharing a vehicle for a new spiritual awakening, a path to become more fully human. The Sister is prioress of the Carmelite Monastery in Indianapolis. Slightly recessed from the street, the monastery rises, a castle evocative of another time and place. A vending truck which has obviously wandered into the wrong driveway, seems anachronistic before this building reminiscent of another gallant age. I half expect a knight on horseback to come trotting up to the front door. Instead, the slight soft-spoken prioress welcomes me into the quiet sanctuary. Here the sisters lead a con-

93

templative life of prayer and study. To support themselves, the women bake altar bread and write and publish books of prayer. Steeped as it is in the stories and ritual of the Catholic Church, you might suspect this community to fiercely preserve tradition, to tolerate no change. Yet tucked in this extraordinarily peaceful refuge, nurtured by reflection and collective living, is a passionate creativity. The sisters bring their femaleness to the Church. Their prayers are gender-inclusive; their rituals are rich with new symbols and images. I am not a Catholic, but to my delightful surprise, I find here, where I least expect it, women I may call sisters in spirit.

Just a few miles down Cold Spring Road sits Al-Fajr Masjid. The mosque houses an Islamic Day School run by another sister of the spirit, Muslimah Mustafah. She and three other Muslim women created the school to teach their children from the heritage of Islam. The students are of different races and cultures. They come from Malaysia, Thailand, Egypt, and Syria. Muslimah suggests that the common experience of motherhood allows women from a plurality of faiths and ethnic backgrounds to come together in ways that can bring about change. "Women have a universal language that makes them less afraid of one another, that enables them to transcend differences and build community."

"The wind blows through all of us and all regions," suggests Gwen Yeaman. I am reminded of my own Jewish tradition which tells me—God is the place of the world, but the world is not God's place. Our rootedness in a particular place connects us to all others in an intricate web that transcends artificial boundaries.

As I interview more and more women, I sense the growth of sacred community. This gathering of women's voices has formed a new chorus, singing in my own soul.

Whether it be the traditional prayer of groups like Women Aglow, an interdenominational Christian women's organization that helps its members have a "closer walk with the Lord" or the seasonal rituals of an eclectic group of women who incorporate female Biblical figures and goddesses into their celebrations of time, Hoosier women make their pilgrimage on the flat land of their Indiana home.

If spirituality does not flap its angel wings in the heavens, but rather is embodied, rooted in experience, then each person's naming of the sacred will reflect his or her journey. In Hebrew one of the names for God is *HaMakom*, the Place. We call God from out of our place, and the place where we stand is holy. Because each calling, each name is a partial apprehension of that spirit, the more names we come to hold, the more places we come to honor, the closer we are to understanding the vast complexity and ultimate singularity of the holy.

As the divine moves through the interior world of women, God becomes known by names other than Father and King. Women call God Mother, Friend, Quilt of Comfort, Living Spring, Womb of Life, Wise Woman, Healer. And as the names for God change, so does the way a woman sees herself as a valuable partner with the divine.

If audacity marks women's newly discovered spiritual voice, humility marks her ancient soul. With an overwhelming sense of life's interconnectedness, women embrace both power and weakness. "Each living thing is the center of the universe, but nothing is central," Gwen Yeaman gives voice to the balance of all life.

As spiritual pilgrims, women know themselves both as creators in the world and as guests on this earth. As creators they seek to birth and midwife, to build and change. As guests, they are ready to receive and sustain, to wonder and offer thanks.

WORLDS OLD AND NEW
Marianne Boruch

Indianapolis, early summer. We're somewhere in the middle of Dvorak's Symphony #9–"from the new world" he said, as an afterthought–finished over a century ago. They're rehearsing all four movements but now it's the slow sad center where rising woodwinds, brass, and timpani give way to the muted strings, a melody, a counter-melody, weave upon weave of a thing past sound and far into longing. These 100 or so musicians are young, mostly in high school, a few in junior high, and a very few even younger than that–a youth orchestra then, the New World Youth Symphony Orchestra, aptly enough. And the sound is amazing really, full and rich and so much larger than this room. But now their conductor, Susan Kitterman, holds up her hand, gesturing *stop stop*, and the held notes fall like rain, the moment awkward, disorienting, the way one wakes from dream. Everyone looks up. Did you hear that? she says to them. Did you hear how beautiful that is? She looks down at the score for a second then back to her young players. That's why we play music, she tells them.

I'm in the doorway, back behind the brass and percussion, nearly deafened sometimes by their sound. Yet the sound carries me. It helps that somewhere in the cello section, my son is part of all this. But I can't think past my joy. I can't put it into words.

◆ ◆ ◆

This particular symphony, Dvorak's ninth, old warhorse that it is, was a stunning accident in 1893, brand new and dumb luck, the result of unabashed enthusiasm one minute, a darker second guessing the next. The Czech composer had been lured to New York for a couple of years to direct the National Conservatory of Music, an experiment, the first tuition-free music school open to all with talent, the first to recruit African-Americans and women. Under Dvorak's influence, its democratic mission was never routine but charged with a deeper fever, American underscored. As a nationalist composer himself, mindful of Czech uneasiness in the all-encompassing Austrian Empire, he readily fell in with the school's founding principles though he seemed, at first, slightly awed by the responsibility. "The Americans expect great things of me," he wrote home his second month here, "and the main thing is, so they say, to show them to the promised land of new and independent art, in short to create a national music. If the small Czech nation can have such musicians, they say, why could not they, too, when their country is so immense." The fact is that he, too, wanted young composers to take up fragments of song from this place, this time though in this country–given our colonial past–the cultural influence to be thrown off was all of Europe, an idea that had seized American writers for some time, Whitman, for instance, calling for literary rebellion, or Emerson, in his elegance, asking the same. Though Dvorak's intent was for the moment pedagogical–"I came to America to discover what young Americans had in them, and to help them to express it"–he got immediately to work on his own version of what might reflect the American heart, or at least his own energy translated by an American experience.

His symphony evolved quickly. Begun in January 1893, it was scored by the end of May, all except the trombone burst at the very end which Dvorak forgot to include until the first rehearsal some months later. It's often said that the raucous beginning echoes the chaotic streets and dockyards of New York. Or perhaps his fascination with trains triggered it, his listening at the railroad bridge over the Harlem River, or from the Bronx hillside he liked early in the day, a particularly fine place to gaze down at his favorite, the express to Chicago, its movement west embodying America to him, that cold-water leap into the new, the spirit dream most loved, oddly, by Europeans who would never leave home, or would return, as he did, keeping faith with the old cities, the forests older than the cities, or the ancient villages with names like *Cermna* and *Zverkovice*. But those mornings, it was all diesel smoke, great clouds of it rising as Dvorak listened, the massive wheels turning, their wheezing and clanging deranged as a bell made, then broken in anger on the forge, the arm raised then coming down until the pitch grew hard and steady as the train got smaller and gave itself to distance, one sound now unless you count the cello sobbing faintly underneath.

◆ ◆ ◆

2:45 at the Athenaeum, any Sunday afternoon. It's break time for the young musicians of the New World Orchestra. Nearly two hours of rehearsal so far, about an hour and a half to go. *I want those eighth notes absolutely staccato*, Susan Kitterman insists once, twice, three times over. It's been at least five runs through the passage in the last twenty minutes, gruelingly difficult because this is no dumbed-down version for kids. The orchestra plays—always—only the complete thing, exactly what each composer has scored. But now it's break, and the instruments are abruptly silenced in their cases or lowered carefully—cellos and string basses—onto their sides to rest on the floor.

Musicians get hungry. At the back of the room is a cornucopia-in-waiting: cookies and carrot cake, vegetables and dip, chips of all persuasion, fruit drinks and soda provided by parents who have signed up for their turn months ago. There's a rush to the tables, paper plates piled high, drinks juggled. The kids wander off in small groups or in couples; individuals find a corner to themselves, pulling out a paperback, the plate balanced on their knees. Two violists, a clarinetist, someone on French horn remain behind for a few minutes, continuing work on a particularly hard measure until they too, put down their instruments and head for the tables. The principal bassoonist is still discussing something with Susan Kitterman, both poised intently over the score.

After a while, the co-principals of the cello section are back at their instruments and it's a kind of quick, joyful pick-up Vivaldi business that starts between them, just for the hell of it. In the corner, a few younger boys at their card game half laugh, half groan over a bad joke that's been making the rounds all afternoon. There are questions for Susan Bever, the orchestra manager, about the rehearsal schedule or a broken music stand or a slipping endpin. Many have ducked out for a moment—quick trips to the restrooms or outside where a small circle of the oldest kids talk softly over their glowing cigarettes. Back inside, near the drinking fountain, two girls show another a letter and watch expectantly as she reads. *Do you believe it?* says one, and they all roll their eyes to the ceiling. But by 3:05, nearly all are back in their seats running through their scales, checking their reeds, tightening their bows and drumheads, working their valves. Like great evil whose mechanics are notoriously banal, this great good is profoundly matter-of-fact. These kids are serious musicians who love to play. And they play. The beauty they make—dark and shining—comes measure by measure. What's extraordinary is how ordinary it all seems.

◆ ◆ ◆

It's probably impossible to figure when Dvorak's New World Symphony was first performed in Indianapolis, but it's surprising how early it could have been. Though records are spotty, depending on programs saved by concert-goers and given to various archives around the city, it's clear that all manner of musical groups were wildly active throughout the nineteenth century. One, in fact, played at the Athenaeum where the New World Youth Orchestra now rehearses, an impressive solid wedding-cake of a building willed into being in the nineties by the rebellious Turners, German immigrants whose culture was mind *and* body, a passionate mix of music and art and athletics. Then called the *Deutsche Haus*—before the anti-German feeling in World War I forced a name change—it hosted that early orchestra, the *Musikverein*, forerunner of the group that still plays. Their music from the period includes Dvorak's *Carnival*, a strange, unruly overture with clashing brass and lovely string work. In 1911, the group changed its name to the Indianapolis Symphony, a move that may have increased its ambition because in 1916 its sixty members did perform and possibly premiere the New World Symphony in Indianapolis. On the religion page, below an article headlined "New Serum to Bring Dead Back to Life," the reviewer at the *Indianapolis Star* was almost as enthusiastic about Dvorak's work, calling it "the most enjoyable feature of the afternoon," though adding—how does one read this?—"but almost an hour was needed to play it."

Other orchestras may have attempted the symphony earlier. By 1895, Karl Schneider had founded his Indianapolis Philharmonic and certainly many visiting groups—the Cincinnati Orchestra, the Chicago Symphony, the Cleveland Orchestra—could have played the work. In 1921 Toscanini managed it, bringing his La Scala Orchestra from Milan for the occasion, one Sunday afternoon in February. The city's major orchestra—The Indianapolis Symphony Orchestra—came to life much later, in 1930, first playing at the Athenaeum, and though the initial seven years of programs are lost, it's certain that Dvorak's piece was performed in 1937 and often after that, a great favorite. By then the ISO was housed at the Murat Theatre, courtesy of the Shriners, whose outrageous taste in architecture was as far away from Dvorak's beloved Bohemia as could be thought or dreamt, their temple modeled after an Islamic mosque, tower and minaret rising up, the whole place cut with terra cotta trim, brown and yellow brick banding, windows of stained glass. And buried within was the Egyptian Room, its motifs drawn from the tombs of the upper Nile, a design planned well before Carter's 1922 discovery of King Tutankhamen's glittering chambers, the image of that glamorous, spooky find raging through the popular imagination of the period. But longing makes for more longing. Perhaps the surreal displacement of Dvorak's music in such a place only deepened the Largo's "beautiful pliant of sorrow confided to the English horn," or so the program note for the earlier 1916 performance put it.

◆ ◆ ◆

My first year out of college I signed on as a full-time searcher of lost books at the University of Chicago's Regenstein Library; a more perfect job I'll never have, mythic and practical all at once. I remember my co-workers: Peter, a tall, quiet kid, a conscientious objector to the Vietnam War, inexplicably assigned to work out his alternative service as a clerk with us. Or mad Sharon, so intent on collecting fines, she'd drive at night on her own time to the addresses on the handwritten bookslips, armed with flashlight to figure out the illegible names and thus—at last, those bastards, she'd gleefully tell us—know who to bill. *Searcher of lost deadbeats*, we called her.

But it's someone else who most comes back to me at odd moments, a fellow searcher slightly older than I was, who talked only of opera. The world stinks and people are rotten, he'd say. But I go home and put on records and hear truth in that singing.

And passion. And real feeling. I loved his saying that, though he troubled me. I'd go home to my tiny one-room apartment and read and try to write until my friends would come by–I didn't have a phone and the foyer doorbell never worked–annoyed because they had to shout up from the street to find me. I thought the opera guy sad and melodramatic and sweet. He dreamed of going to live in Italy–Milan probably–where everyone, he said, was wild for opera, not like here. I used to stare at him when he wasn't looking, watch him as he stood momentarily shuffling through the small cards we searchers carried. It's just that he could so easily step from this world into another. For all that singing, there was a kind of silence around him as he worked at the monster card catalog or walked the stacks.

◆ ◆ ◆

"You just came off this really sentimental violin line," Susan Kitterman is telling the clarinets at rehearsal, "and now you're the voice of reason." It's a playful, no-nonsense moment, just when everyone was dreaming off, caught in the flight of the crescendo. Some of the kids nod, others lean forward and scribble something on their music, a few half smile at her remark. It's an astonishing new thought to me, the notion that this music isn't just a wash of lovely, compelling sound but as complicated, as unpredictable as conversation, that one instrument answers another, one might even parody itself. Two might argue, one sober, one drunk; one is forgiving, one refuses; one knows only the simplest things, one loves the shadow world and won't give up its sad delirium, ever.

It slowly occurs to me that this isn't just some romantic (interpretation?) foisted on a play of notes; I've actually begun to hear differently, not music at a distance but close up, how it's made, how it rises and falls, cuts itself off, stubbornly repeats itself, goes inward, turning a minor key, bursting out again with its shift back

to major, into the bright world. And I wonder if what I'm beginning to hear in music is close to what I'm always wanting in poems, a way inward but at the same time, a way to love the world's complexity. Or maybe not to love or even to understand it really–is that ever possible?–but to co-exist with it. Except to invite more of music's complication into poems–how exactly to do that? One varies syntax; one moves in and out of memory; one whispers or one's emphatic. *But what does it sound like?* I want to say about any poem I read, any poem I try to write. Because that's where the secret reveals itself. It takes such patience, this spirit life; Dvorak's saying once that art is simply an elaboration on the smallest things we notice. Susan Kitterman is hard on these kids, exacting. "Bite the strings!" she calls out to the second violins. Then, waving everyone to stop, "You know what? I think you ought to practice this at home." "A low blow," Susan Bever whispers next to me. But she begins again, working the passage over and over. "This is very, very tricky" she tells them. "You want that feeling of reaching farther than you really can."

◆ ◆ ◆

All that American winter of 1893, while he worked on his famous symphony, Dvorak was obsessed with going home for the summer to his country place in Vysoka, far from Prague. Slowly though, as spring came with all green things stirring, he was caught by another idea. Inviting his whole family to join him in America he would make the trip from New York to rural Spillville, Iowa, a Czech immigrant community, where, he was promised, his language was spoken right on the street. He had, just a couple of weeks earlier, put the finishing touches on his symphony "from the new world." Now he was speeding west through part of that world–Pennsylvania, then Ohio, then Indiana–on the very train he loved to watch from a distance in New York. There was a brief stop at Fort Wayne. Maybe Dvorak stepped out on to the platform to buy sandwiches because someone decided everyone was hungry. About a hundred and forty miles south, in Indianapolis, no doubt there were kids just being kids who would grow up to become string, woodwind, and brass players, and, since the Indianapolis Symphony Orchestra at first recruited locally, it would be their fortunate lot to perform this piece so recently put to paper, the one still running through Dvorak's head, waking him up at night.

It's perhaps too easy to go omniscient and follow this movie back quickly, like one of those time-lapsed films that rush the seed into flower and then, in reverse, play its flourishing back to the merest speck. This isn't thought, of course. It's reverie. 1893, and Dvorak continues nevertheless on to Spillville and its facts, to a summer spent discovering the scarlet tanager, inviting its song into his music, or listening to his six children at play, or taking over the organ at St. Wenislaus for early mass, working afternoons on an amazing quartet, later dubbed his most "American," and thus its name—"three months," he wrote home, "which will remain a happy memory for the rest of our lives." But part of the real dream is its specifically American darkness. "Few people and a great deal of empty space," he wrote back to a friend in Bohemia ". . . and it is very 'wild' here and sometimes very sad—sad to despair. But habit is everything."

Meanwhile, I think past Dvorak's part in the movie to these imagined facts: 1893, and of those kids in Indianapolis, say one will play—how many years from now?—the difficult English horn solo in the Largo which dips and turns and opens into the brain's most secret part which remembers odd detail and feels its chill. She's twelve; it's beginning to rain. From the porch, she notices that back in the house her brother's voice is changing. It's funny, cracking on the word *crocus*. Or she hears how rain floods the wooden gutters,

a pulse in that somehow, a low heartbeat. And what about this?—that downtown, three young violinists who will someday press and rage and release themselves to pure flight in Dvorak's third movement are now sitting cross-legged in the dirt at the edge of Michigan Street, under the rough lean-to that carpenters have slapped together, watching the new *Deutsche Haus* go up. One's bored out of his mind. But one kid loves how the canvas tarp billows out, the workmen shouting and whistling and reaching hard to pull it over the enormous hoard of brick and lumber because of the rain, because the wind's so fierce, the whole business blurring—Dvorak's Iowa to Indiana to right now, this moment. Why not? Everything's so all at once finally. And is it music or poetry that such confusion isn't chaos but some vast complexity I can barely begin to grasp?

In my old Catholic neighborhood in Chicago, we used to hear about the contemplatives, certain orders of nuns we never saw, cloistered away somewhere. The idea seemed scary and attractive and weird. Then we heard about the holy rumble, their job only to pray, words rushed like music, something near chant. And one of our teachers told us—Sister Norbertus or Sister Mary Hubertine?—that this sacred hum, exactly this, kept the earth turning on its axis, not merely this day or this minute, but for all worlds of the past and the future because life is linked and there are no divisions in time. It's plain fact, she told us with nary a blink, like science is fact.

For proof, she instructed us to close our eyes and listen hard. And she was right. We could hear them. The world was linked. That low-grade roar locked in our heads, steady undercurrent of rushing blood and flashing nerve—was it only that? Maybe it was those women after all, pulling from the world its oldest sound, every dark and light in the universe subdued, backdrop to thought, to words, to laughter, to every sorrow coming up slowly, inevitably, a forewarning or a reminder. Certain moments, if I become very still, even now I hear it. And I think about Dvorak, falling asleep those nights in Spillville, haunted by the symphony he's finished and set aside, its last ghost notes settling back to their first nothing. But it isn't nothing.

◆ ◆ ◆

Sometimes I wander around the Athenaeum while the kids in the New World rehearse. I can sit easily enough in the back of the small auditorium where they play, dragging in a folding chair, and occasionally I do. Or I can join the handful of parents not from Indianapolis, who, like me, come long distances to get here, waiting out the afternoon in the lobby on the plush benches that circle the large pillars keeping the high ceiling at bay. Gone are the original Turners who came long ago from Germany, but down the hall are old photographs, little doors to elsewhere, turn-of-the-century water-stained shots of a singing class, of the lower school, of the kindergarten whose tiny charges have dropped their hands into a table of sand while their teacher stares blankly out into the future.

It's dark in that hallway but I'm always surprised at the next photograph, how enormous and busy it is, blown-up and hand colored to make an August night stay forever. *Ox-Barbecue*, the caption says, 1952, two years after I was born. Table after table set up in the Athenaeum's biergarten out back, the waiters in white jackets, it's way past dusk, little lights hanging from the trees, castor plants and 4 o'clocks lining the dance floor, the band nearly blurring, instruments mid-air. These are the children and grandchildren of those who built this place and so many are dancing, so many still at the tables, leaning this way and that over their plates to catch something said under the music, the end of a joke, a crucial bit of story. I always figure that if I counted the dancers, then the vacant chairs at the tables, I'd come out even. But if I move abruptly, to the opposite wall, there's a more curious juxtaposition—another photograph, same place, the biergarten blown-up huge and hand colored again, this time with nothing in it at all, the band shell empty, the bare expanse of the dance floor oddly, suddenly austere. Only the big-fisted castor plants remain, rows of 4 o'clocks languid and zinnia straight up in the planters set along the walk. And I like to think that if I squinted hard at the crowded version, then turned quick and stared, I could call up those dancers, superimpose them, bring them back, flushed and expectant, out of that stilled August air.

◆ ◆ ◆

Everything written about Dvorak's 9th Symphony—his new world—eventually comes back to a kind of ache in the piece, human and inevitable, coming up most profoundly in the Largo, its famous second movement. And the origin of that sorrow? Some call up African-American spirituals or Native-American rhythms, both of which Dvorak praised and even suggested as heavily influencing the music before turning back on the notion, to claim his homeland—Bohemian melodies—once again as his real spiritual source. But finally, if we believe his letters or his friends' reminiscences, it's a long, abiding homesickness that floods this work written in New York that winter and spring of 1893, too far from his garden in Vysoka, his pigeons there, his favorite card game, *danka*, his walks with family and friends. Elements in folksong of whatever cultural stripe might call up the feel of a lost time and place. Certainly the Largo in particular, its simple, plaintive lines of melody in spite of the elaborate and careful orchestration, moves in ways that awaken melancholy in us. Maybe that's the poetry in Dvorak's method, his use of the folksong's pentatonic scale with its odd minor seventh, a half step up or down, a private hesitation where one might expect only the major's full step, self-assured public sound; or the habit of returning over and over to a note, tonic

100

or dominant, the sense of the elegiac in that lyric repetition, a looking back that weighs heavier and heavier.

"Goin' Home," of course, is the shorthand name of the Largo's memorable theme, an actual song culled from the symphony by William Arms Fisher, Dvorak's former student from the National Conservatory, after the composer's death in 1904. Endlessly popular in the first third of this century, it was a staple in the piano repertoire of most middle-class homes though in my family, where irreverence was almost a hobby, the piece, at least in my mother's childhood, had a more practical use. So thoroughly recognized was "Goin' Home" by friends and acquaintances in the twenties that if an afternoon visitor began to overstay her welcome, a sign from my grandmother—maybe her little finger touched her eyebrow—would send my mother to the piano to launch a small performance. "Some took the hint," my grandmother remarked dryly to me years later, "some didn't." Not that this story ever altered the melody's power for her. Though it became a family tale I loved, I think in fact my grandmother told it as personal camouflage, a way to balance, maybe even deny, the embarrassingly deep effect the piece had on her. Those summers I stayed with her as a child, I listened as she played the song sometimes, late afternoon, though occasionally she'd stop, overcome for a moment, before picking up the next measure, a slip neither she nor I ever spoke of. I wonder now what lost time or place the piece recalled for her, what moment she had buried which, because of some delicious, minor turn of sound, came up quick to stop her.

So music rewards us with its abundant sorrow, a curious form of happiness, or poetry does, or any art which stills and darkens even as it gives us the shining world. That Dvorak's piece continues to move us is perhaps not a large miracle but a small one, this music so threatened by familiarity, an orchestral cliché by now, certainly one of the greatest hits, this crowd pleaser from its first performance in Carnegie Hall where even that sophisticated audience willfully misbehaved, interrupting with wild applause after the second movement, shouting *Dvorak! Dvorak!* until he shyly rose from the back shadows of his box.

The work's continuing pull might be its peculiarly American feel, written as it was in the uneasy half light between cultures. Dvorak as outsider, as immigrant—for the duration of its writing at least—plays out a universal American experience, all those deeply solitary elements in us that don't quite fit no matter how long our families have been here, or what our circumstance. That our connection to place, to anything really, is finally a spiritual act, an act of will and imagination, not mere accident of biology or history, may be at the heart of all this. It's true that the Athenaeum, with its biergarten and rathskeller so lovingly reproduced, went up as a kind of wish to bring the old world here, a Bavarian castle grafted solidly on new world swamp and prairie. And for that, its longing is the longing of Dvorak's Largo, a homesickness. But that dramatic juxtaposition moves the imagination forward as well as back, an heroic nerve in that, as if one could really live there, in the future, as if there was a plan, howbeit close to dream.

◆ ◆ ◆

It's the long drive home to West Lafayette that I dread, especially after the occasional late rehearsals that stretch into evening. Everyone is tired. Going over Dvorak's lively scherzo, Susan Kitterman calls out "I don't want it beautiful, I want it feverish," and there's one last fierce electric upping of energy in the room. "Good," she says, "good. We're doing wonderfully." But now the kids are packing up, putting away their music stands. Some still joke and talk, the brass players especially refusing to give up, giddy with exhaustion, launching impromptu into Ain't Misbehavin'.

"Go home already!" a violinist yells over to them, laughing. My son is worn out, I can tell; the cello case takes both arms now. It seems enormous, bigger than before; he's listing to one side as he steers it through the crowd of parents come to pick up their kids.

I may dread the drive but I look forward to my son's stories of who said what outrageous thing, his delight at certain parts of the music—did you hear that neat place in the Dvorak, he asks, where it's just a string quartet playing? He's flipping the dial on our radio until something stops him. We argue about it—is it Mozart or Haydn? I'm sure it's Mozart, he says.

It's late but because of that, it's cooler now and we decide to take back roads, not I-65 but 421, then over on 28. We'll avoid the construction that way, and driving a little slower, we can open the windows, the fields giving off their sweetness—something's just been cut. One of Beethoven's late quartets comes on, one he wrote after he'd gone totally deaf. I turn to tell my son this, but he's fallen asleep. It's dark by now, the fields black but wild with fireflies doing their slow blink off and on.

There's a bit near the end of Dvorak's Largo—maybe my favorite part—where everything drops down to nothing for a measure or two, not even one violin or the small whistling of a flute keeps the momentum. It's startling, this happening once. But it happens again not much later, and then a third time, long enough that each pause deepens to a genuine absence—eerie, this widening hole in the music. I never know quite what to make of it, or of the pleasure it brings. Everything held back suddenly, the world beyond—a rich, grave silence—offering itself like that.

102

Works Consulted

Beckerman, Michael. *Dvorak and His World*. Princeton, N.J.: Princeton University Press, 1993.

Dvorak, Antonin. *Symphonies, Nos. 8 and 9 in Full Score*. New York: Dover, 1984.

Hampl, Patricia. *Spillville*. Minneapolis: Milkweed Editons, 1987.

Hughes, Gervase. *Dvorak: His Life and Music*. New York : Dodd, Mead, 1967.

Fischl, Viktor. *Antonin Dvorak: His Achievement*. Westport, Conn.: Greenwood Press, 1970.

Sourek, Otakar. *Antonin Dvorak: Letters & Reminiscences*. New York: Da Capo, 1984.

——. The Orchestral Works of Antonin Dvorak. Prague: Artia, 1957.

Tibbetss, John C. *Dvorak in America, 1892-1895*. Portland, Oregon: Amadeus Press, 1993.

Many thanks to David Lewis, Archival Librarian at the Indiana State Library in Indianapolis, to Barbara Mondary at the IUPUI Library, and to Dorothy Linke and Mabel Webb at the Athenaeum for their help. This essay, in altered form, appeared in The Iowa Review, *winter 1997.*

SOULS IN SOLITARY COMMUNION
David Hoppe

When I was a teenager, I used to love going for late night walks along the deserted streets of my suburban burg. The nighttime was much better for walking than the day. By day the streets seemed wider and even though most of the houses were occupied by toiling Moms, they looked locked up, abandoned. In my hometown, in the daytime, being on the street was a left-out or guilty feeling. It made you wonder why you weren't somewhere else—in school, at a job, a camp or with friends. At night, on the other hand, the houses crouched closer to the curb, casting intimate blue shadows over lawns and driveways. Though mostly dark, the houses still expressed an aura of habitation that was missing before sundown. Part of this was thanks to sleep's vital stillness, the hum of dreams. And part was due to the phosphorescent glow spilling from one isolated window and then another; the alpha light of souls in solitary communion.

It is still like this. When I take my dog walking through our Indianapolis neighborhood at night, I cannot help but be impressed by the prevalence of this suburban trinity: single family dwellings, cars, and, through one window after another, the multi-color flux and sparkle of television light. At times I can see the screens so clearly it seems my unknown neighbors intend for strangers like myself to share their viewing. It is tempting to stop and watch—not the people in their houses, but what they are watching.

Which begs the question, I know, of what it is I—we—are looking at. McLuhan pointed out that it's the medium itself, not the message that matters. In general I believe this is true.

But this is a generality made up of a blizzard of particulars. What makes me weep will likely send you to the kitchen for a snack. This is the key to electronic virtuality: although a single medium has gathered us together, our individuality is left intact, indeed, is accentuated, albeit in ways compatible with a mass marketplace. If you haven't found a progam suited to your own set of vulnerabilites yet, keep looking, keep looking.

The paradox represented by this fluid yet uneasy relationship between the mass and the particular accounts for why many of TV's most maudlin, least compelling moments come when it deliberately attempts to play community organizer. From the operatic bathos of Jerry Lewis's annual Labor Day Telethons to the self-important speculations of network pundits on election night, TV is most like a parody of itself when it contrives to convey a message intended to "bring us together." In spite of TV's massive reach, "us" is a concept decidedly subordinate to a dependent "I."

Although for a variety of reasons, from the crassly commercial to the democratically spiritual, television boosters prefer to define their medium by those occasions when it has seemingly distilled the nation's attention—the unfolding drama, say, of John Kennedy's assasination combined with the subsequent on-air murder of Lee Harvey Oswald, and then the dead president's funeral procession—such instances are not representative. Like most aspects of life, we remember what is uncommon. And, for better or worse, what is uncommon does not stand replication.

This helps account for the success of cable revival programming like Nick at Nite—an entire network dedicated to bringing back "vintage" shows, reruns of programs from the 1950s, '60s, and '70s. Here not the uncommon, but the everyday experience of television is revisited. Lucy, Rob, and Laura and the Munsters are presented not in a museum or via some chopped-up "special," but uncut and regularly scheduled in their natural habitat. TV, for the first time, with cross-generational continuity. I am not only watching programs I remember seeing at my grandparents' house, my son is watching them, too.

This conflation of television's past and present lends dimension to an experience that was once easily dismissed as being, by definition, superficial. An adult in my own time and place, I find myself staring into the eletronic visage of my parents' desires, delusions, evasions, and ideals. In short, what I see here are the tracks of their mortality and, by a short stretch, my own. Irony, the viewer's knowing defense against the seductions and indignities of the video marketplace, frays at the edge of this revelation.

Maybe this fascination with television is attributable to my suburban upbringing. Had I been brought up in a dramatic landscape, dominated by mountains, the sea, or, for that matter, skyscraper canyons and urban rumble, I might have experienced a larger, unifying power in the sense of place. But where I lived the earth was flat, most of the trees were tied down to keep them from blowing away. Our houses, while not all alike, were of a kind, they differed by degrees. This suburbia was a world made safe for a fantasy of manageable children. A world, in many ways, that was an extension of, rather than a counterforce to, television.

No wonder then that when, as an adult, I finally arrived in Indianapolis, I felt at home. While considerably older than the post-World War II development where I grew up, Indianapolis was never really an urban place. Residential in character, its center was not the congested hive of habitation and commerce that typified the early lives of America's major cities. Where in these places suburban development followed means of transport—in most cases, the trolley car—Indianapolis seems to have been averse to crowding from the very start. The house, not the apartment, was always the standard. Neither fully urban nor rural, Indianapolis was and is, in its passive/aggressive way, a suburban community.

And, some would claim, a community of churches. There are fourteen pages of church listings in the Yellow Pages—and these don't include synagogues, Buddhist, or Muslim temples. More pages than one finds for more worldly, if unconventional, ministries like psychologists or taverns or shopping malls. But organized religion has never spoken to my spiritual proclivities, another consequence, I suspect, of my suburban worldview.

For the religious institution's place in a suburban world has always seemed uneasy to me. Suburbs are, by definition, exercises in avoidance behavior. They are organized efforts to put a variety of urban issues—from crowding to crime—at arm's length in favor of a materialistic individualism. This, in my experience, puts institutionalized spiritualism in the unwelcome position of being the village nag, forever trying to remind people that there is something more to life than what they spend their lives trying to acquire: houses, yards, cars—and television sets.

This, of course, is a jaundiced view. It doesn't take into account either the fulfillments of being part of a community or the comforts provided by faith in times of trauma and loss. But as a suburbanite—one who has lived most of my life placing an almost sacred premium on privacy and who, as far as loss is concerned, is more or less resigned to its dumb, staring inevitability—I'll take my comfort wherever and whenever I can find it.

In my life I've visited more types of spiritual practice than most people I know: I've been present at Quaker meetings and gospel rave-ups; Pentecostal testifying and Catholic mass; I've gone to Temple on Friday night, sat with Buddhists and wrestled over ideas with Unitarians. When I was a teenager, a Presbyterian minister counseled me about conscientious objection; a member of the Universal Life Church read Sir Thomas Browne on harmonics at my first wedding; a Lutheran pastor presided over my second; and a Rabbi counseled my wife and me on spiritual questions prior to the birth of our son who, by the way, is named after Graham Greene, great Church of England drop-out and haunted Catholic convert.

These brushes with various traditions have all made me reflect and wonder. None have made me well up, though, the way I did during last night's dream sequence about a murdered son on NYPD Blue.

Much as I might hate to admit it, it is television that has provided me with the sort of quotidian solace, revelation, and recognition that I associate with spiritual pathways. This is not to say that I consider TV a fount of wisdom. What I find there is just as likely to repulse or, worse, degrade me as it is of setting something free. The same thing, though, might be said about other varieties of spiritual experience.

I am well aware of the many raps on television. I don't disagree with most of those I can think of. Television, as it has been developed in the United States, is a blatantly commercial medium, an ongoing electronic museum of capitalistic expression, if not art. Much of what it does is aimed at creating the kind of personal insecurity in those of us who watch which can only be addressed through purchase of the things that pay for the programs in the first place. Self-referential to the core, TV only asks us questions which it can answer in its own magically materialistic terms.

As the automobile transformed the American countryside, so television has undoubtedly twisted our psychic landscape. I can only leave it to those whose experience spans the time before TV and after to describe the way life without it may have been. As a member of the first generation to live in a television society, I can rail against the machine but I can only imagine another kind of community. One, perhaps, in which there are no single-family dwellings, let alone no TVs—a place where we really do have to live together. Or I can try to inhabit my suburban world as best I can, which may include accepting forms of spiritual comfort from some unlikely, unexpected sources.

If the symbiotic relationship between suburbia and the automobile is, by now, a commonplace of American social observation, suburbia's relationship with television should be as readily acknowledged. As I have already suggested, the very characteristics that make TV seem spiritually alienating from urban and rural points of view—its tendency, for example, to replace communities associated with the street or the village green with the virtual community of "Televisionland"—fit the contours of suburban sensibility like a Perfect Sleeper mattress.

So here I am. Disconcerted by this place but suited for it. We are, I believe, spiritual animals—unable, for all our avoiding, to escape our nature. Who, though, would have thought that nature might take so many forms? Or that our ability to create new forms, from the residential geometries of suburbia to lines of resolution, would be this capacious?

Through the brightened windows of the houses on my street I glimpse signs of private ritual. A basketball game, coming in live from the west coast in one; a dark-haired woman's face, frankly beckoning in another. It has been suggested that theater (through ritual, a kind of church) is meant to help us collective-

105

108

110

///

CHARITY
Alyce Miller

The summer I was seventeen, I flew from Cleveland to Indianapolis to work as a volunteer tutor for the American Friends' Service Committee. I had just graduated from high school, though on principle refused to attend the ceremony, what I considered a display of excessive bourgeois sentimentality. I was angst-ridden, restless, appropriately morose, and generally pessimistic about the state of the world.

I hadn't lived at home since my sophomore year of high school, and that final summer before I was to start college, my parents and I tacitly agreed that we would all be better off if I occupied myself with something meaningful—at a distance. So I ditched my old waitressing job in favor of the American Friends' Service Committee, a Quaker organization with summer work camps in target cities where urban poverty had taken its toll.

The idea held appeal. My parents were strong proponents of social activism: anti-Vietnam demonstrations (my father took me to the Moratorium in Washington, D.C.) and sit-ins for civil rights. Over the years, they'd encouraged me to tutor children in inner-city Cleveland (the area known as Hough) as well as disadvantaged children in the lower grades of the public schools. I even had the idea (when I wasn't envisioning myself as a female William Kuntsler in a court room defending Black Panthers) that I might someday be a teacher at an alternative school for poor kids. Having always attended racially and economically integrated schools, I came to believe that education could be the great equalizer, that the only discrepancy between advantage and disadvantage was equal access to knowledge and imagination.

My parents are old-fashioned liberals, full believers in the equality of all people, generous toward others, and conservative, even spartan, in their own personal lives. They are also deeply and quietly religious. It seems perfectly logical that my parents, before joining the Episcopal church when I was a kid, flirted with the Quakers, whose philosophy of nonviolence meshed with my parents' own world view. I can still picture the unembellished Quaker meeting house in Ann Arbor, Michigan, with its hard, stiff-backed wooden benches and lack of adornment, where people greeted one another quietly and warmly, and then spent long periods of worship in silence. My own religious interests tend now to be driven more by philosophical and academic curiosity than by acts of faith, though for one brief period in my teens I believed fervently in God.

I have the Episcopal church to thank, during the volatile and explosive sixties, for a strong social conscience and the belief that you do unto others as you would want them to do unto you—compassion, empathy, generosity—in a word, charity. From my seventeen-year-old perspective, the world was deeply troubled and badly in need of change. I was both a cynic and an idealist. I boarded the plane to Indianapolis that summer with mixed motives. For all my good intentions, I was also a teenager about to be in a new city on my own without parental supervision.

The afternoon I flew into Indianapolis I was thrilled to be out of Ohio, and turned hopeful and upbeat, if not a tad arrogant, about my anticipated mission in Indianapolis. I basked in the vague idea that I had the power to change the lives of "the less fortunate" because I knew how to empathize, or "relate," as we said back then.

But I also was equally aware, class and economic divisions being what they are, that it was patronizing to assume I was the only one with something to give. I should probably mention here that the AFSC sent volunteers only to those communities that "invited" them and that while most of us on this particular project were from out of state, we were to work very closely with community liaisons from the area.

The AFSC was founded in 1917 in order that conscientious objectors could help civilian victims during World War I. The purpose was to promote both peace and the assumption that "all life is sacred." The AFSC has a long history of social advocacy for the disempowered: the hungry, the poor, the homeless, and the unemployed, both nationally and internationally. In 1938, for example, the AFSC arranged emigration and resettlement for Jewish families living in Nazi-occupied Germany. In 1965 it worked to integrate previously all-white schools in the South. In keeping with the Quaker ethos, the AFSC was out in the world, honoring humanity and the dignity and potential of every individual.

George Fox, who founded the Quakers (the Society of Friends), wrote, in the manner of I Corinthians, in 1694: "The Lord showed me, so that I did see clearly, that he did not dwell in these temples which men had commanded and set up, but in people's hearts . . . his people were his temple, and he dwelt in them."

There were a dozen of us teenage volunteers who had flown in from the East and Midwest to spend our summer in the basement of the Mary Rigg Center on Morris Street, just a couple blocks south of Rhodius Park. We arrived with minimal possessions and spent our days planning and volunteering. In the evenings we had "free time," which we passed either talking, shooting pool, going for ice cream, or walking through the neighborhood. We divided up domestic duties like cooking and laundry and cleaning. We slept on cots (girls in one room, boys in another) and showered gang style. Like most of the other volunteers, I'd brought only one small duffel bag. I had two pairs of jeans, several changes of underwear and socks, a pair of sneakers and a pair of sandals, a pair of cut-offs, and a few T-shirts. Oh, and my jean jacket with the cannibas leaf patch on one arm and the Black Power fist patch on the other. I'd brought a few books too: Herman Hesse, Eldridge Cleaver, Marcus Garvey, Stan Steiner, and Vine Deloria, Jr.

It was terrifically hot and humid that summer, and even the box fans we had going in the basement did little to dispel the oppressive heat. Our tempers ran short, and some of us got along better than others. Everyone tended to stay up late because it was too humid to sleep. Some of us would go out and roam around until the air cooled, but the neighborhood wasn't considered "all that safe," and we were urged to be cautious, particularly two of the other volunteers and me.

B and C, from Philadelphia, and I formed a trio. We got dibs on the tutoring and then signed up for laundering detail to insure that we would always be together. Our combination was particularly volatile because B and C were black and I am white, and many of the neighborhood's inhabitants were not pleased by their presence, or by our friendship. Even some of the other volunteers took a dim view of our liaison. B was tall and broad-shouldered, with the beginnings of a goatee and mustache. He was very protective toward C and me when we walked around, always insisting on taking the outside of the sidewalk. If a car slowed or we were passing a group of young white men in the park, he went on red alert. We had bottles tossed at us a few times and some racial slurs slung from car windows. Over and over we were counseled by the AFSC staff to be careful, but we refused to stay sequestered in the center as they suggested.

116

In the evening, B and C and I staked out our turf on the stairwell leading up to the parking lot where we would talk until the wee hours of the morning. B and I smoked Camel nonfilters we pooled our change to buy. He and C had come together from the alternative school they attended in Philadelphia. It turned out none of us had "worked out" in public school, a factor which I'm sure drew us together and made us more sympathetic to our young charges.

Twice a week, after tutoring, we dragged large canvas bags of all the volunteers' clothes down Morris Street to the laundromat and sat up on the hot dryers, sweating and joking while the clothes spun. We became inseparable. B appointed himself our "play brother" and took his role seriously. Back home he belonged to a street gang called Sons of Soul, where he was known as Krazy. C went by the nickname Snoopy. They decided I needed a nickname too, and one night after I put away a whole Sara Lee strawberry cheesecake on my own, I became known as Cheesecake.

Each of the AFSC volunteers took on different roles in the community. One boy built a beautiful set of playground equipment from wood and discarded tires. Another helped people clean up their yards. B and C and I ran the tutoring program for young neighborhood children, a task we set about with fierce determination. C, in particular, was very committed. She was a beautiful girl with chocolate skin and a gigantic curly Afro. Her earnestness was infectious, and B and I threw our hearts and souls into getting things set up. All the children were elementary school age, and almost all came from dirt poor families (not unlike B's and C's). Reading materials were donated, and we worked to stretch the workbooks and pens and pencils and paper among all our charges. In fact, a bulk of materials was generously donated by a Catholic nun who, I can't help but recall, greeted me at her front door a few blocks away dressed in a two-piece bathing suit when I came to pick up the boxes.

We divided the children among ourselves and combined individual tutoring with group activities. The children were often inconsistent about coming, and we could have as few as two children on some days and as many as ten on others. My two regulars were Junior and Richard, neither of whom ever missed a day. Junior lived close by in a ramshackle house with older siblings and a mother. Junk cars were parked all over the front yard. His older brother ran an auto repair business of sorts and his teenage sister mostly hung out on the porch with her baby on her hip waiting for her boyfriend. Junior was tow-headed, with startling blue eyes, a handsome, sweet-natured child who liked coming around the center. Richard was one of the few black kids, a gorgeous boy the color of bittersweet chocolate, often shy and reserved.

As the summer wore on, I became aware that the strained countenances of the children as we practiced reading and writing often signaled a gentle tolerance for our clumsy efforts to teach them "skills" and "expose" them to experiences beyond the confines of Morris Street. When I look back, I realize the poor kids were probably bored to death, but like all kids, they craved attention, and it didn't matter in what form that attention came. Soon we began to add field trips to our program and took them to the art museum, the larger parks, and the zoo.

Nevertheless, a lot of the children showed up only sporadically, despite the fact that we came in a large van to retrieve them for their parents' convenience. I remember in particular two little chubby girls with scraggly blonde hair and raggedy clothes, who were always cheerful and exuberant, but who more often than not were kept at home by their anxious mother who would tell me through the broken screen door in a voice barely above a whisper, "I need them today. They can't come."

What she needed them for she never said, and I despaired for

117

the girls who would be kept inside their rundown little house with the television blaring. But, on the other hand, as C and I discussed, why should this mother turn her daughters over to strangers? On the days the girls did come, they had a great time, and when we'd drop them off we'd always ask the mother if we could expect them the next day. She smiled and nodded, but the next day she'd change her mind.

There was never any open resistance, but I often sensed tentativeness and suspicion on the part of many parents. Even as varied as our group was, we came from "outside." We didn't look or dress or talk like people from the neighborhood. And we were taking their children away.

In the staff meetings, there was often an expressed frustration among the volunteers that something they had said or done was being misunderstood or some offer of generosity was refused. There was also the specter of racism toward B and C (also frankly shared by a couple of the volunteers), and the unanswerable question of whether or not some of the reluctance by parents was fueled by racial prejudice.

There were the neighborhood parents who, seemingly pleased we were doing nice things for the community, simply did not want their children going off with B and C to be tutored, because they didn't like blacks, and a small scandal erupted when it was rumored that B was himself only functionally literate. This was partially true, though B was smart as a whip and terrific and loving with the kids. Spelling, mostly, was not his strong suit. But as I already said, tutoring was ironically the least of what we did.

That summer was in many ways a turning point in my life. I would like to write here that I flew into Indianapolis, an eager and idealistic young woman with a heart overflowing with love, and through tenacious effort miraculously transformed the lives of poverty-stricken, underprivileged children through the gift of reading. I would like to say

that Junior and Richard stayed in touch over the years and while their older brothers went off to jail and their sisters got pregnant, both ended up going to college and, against all odds, graduating with honors and winning scholarships to professional schools. In this scenario, Junior would become a doctor and Richard a lawyer, and they would return to their neighborhood and act as role models and inspiration for a new generation.

But there is no way of knowing what we achieved that summer. The narrative is simple: we came for three months and then we left. In the fall, I went on to college. B and C returned to Philadelphia to finish high school. Within a year C was pregnant by her married alternative high school mentor who promised to take her to Brazil (which he eventually did, bringing to light yet another wife). B finished high school and got a job. He wasn't much of a letter writer, and so beyond that, I don't know what became of him.

A century and a half ago French novelist George Sand remarked almost brutishly, "Charity degrades those who receive it and hardens those who dispense it." Maybe she is half right, and certainly her words take on a contemporary ring as we watch the complicated transformation of welfare into something called workfare. What is charity? Who is being served by acts of charity? Is charity, in essence, an oxymoron, working in direct opposition to itself? What is being given and what is being received?

Contrary to what Sand might say, I wasn't hardened by my experience at all, and I don't think B and C were either. I know that I learned a lot that summer. But the truth is that more often than not the tutoring sessions were dull and painful, the kids restless, and the air so thick we all would have had more fun swimming. Even with my good intentions I didn't really know how to teach kids to read, and resorted to schoolmarmish tactics they put up with because they probably didn't know they had a choice.

I have no idea how our short presence in the neighborhood actually affected anyone in the long term, nor what effect our subsequent departure had. I do remember Junior and I separated in tears, because we truly liked each other, but that is all. I knew when I said good-bye to him and Richard that we would never see each other again. I would return to my world and they to theirs. I was almost a legal adult about to enter college and they had years of childhood and adolescence to get through.

Over the summer, in that intense heat, I became aware of the double edge of charity, the arrogance that often accompanies generosity, the assumptions we tried to fight while remaining observant and questioning. Add to that all the complicated class-centric dynamics of helping those who have not had "advantages." Of course we had the support of immediate community leaders, and were welcomed warmly. Yet I kept thinking how if we came "bearing gifts," the gift was our privilege. And privilege is a fact of chance, not a function of choice. That summer I often wondered why my presence should be any more significant than anyone else's. This is not a condemnation of community work, nor is it in any way a criticism of the AFSC. I'm simply suggesting that, in general, altruism is never as simple as it seems.

Even B and C, who were underprivileged themselves, were by their very association with AFSC viewed as "advantaged." While the rest of us had paid to come volunteer (part of the donation), B and C had received "scholarships." (Months after the AFSC, I went to visit B and C in Philadelphia for two weeks. They both lived in ghetto neighborhoods, B in a tenement with a dirt floor in the kitchen. Both their respective living conditions were as substandard as those of many of the poor whites we'd worked with in Indianapolis.)

Last spring, early in the evening, I drove up from Bloomington to find the neighborhood where I worked that summer, twenty some-odd years before. I've lived two years now in Indiana, having spent all my adult life in the San Francisco Bay Area. I never expected to return here. When I left Indianapolis that summer, it had been one summer of my life; that was all.

After moving back here, I often thought of my three months with the AFSC. I scoured a map of Indianapolis to see if street names jogged my memory. I couldn't even remember the name of the center where we'd lived. The one thing I did recognize was Rhodius Park, where B and C and I liked to go and swing and harmonize and ponder the human condition and the state of the world. It was in Rhodius Park that B, the ever-protective "big brother," confided to me, almost in tears, that C was having an affair with her married teacher back in Philadelphia, and he didn't know what to do about it. And it was in Rhodius Park that C told me in strictest confidence that B was not eighteen as he claimed and looked to be, but was only thirteen and a half! We couldn't tell anyone because the AFSC would have sent him home immediately. These secrets drew us closer.

It was about six o'clock in the evening when I drove up to Indianapolis with the intention of tracing the way to Rhodius Park as a starting point. I had an eerie feeling that I should be experiencing a kind of déjà vu, but nothing was connecting for me. I could have been anywhere. There was no flash of recognition, no flood of memories. The park seemed small and innocuous. The shape of the neighborhood was nothing like what I remembered. I circled the block and cut back across Morris Street. A low-slung brick building came into view, looking vaguely familiar, but only because I had my eyes peeled for it. The sign out front said "Mary Rigg Center." Even that didn't ring a bell, but the building itself seemed appropriately located. Around back was a parking lot, where I pulled in. On the second floor through the open doors into a gymnasium I could see kids in red and blue smocks playing an organized game of basketball. A couple of adults were officiating. All but one of the players were white. All but one were boys. Lots of cheering came from inside. There was the steady rhythm of feet pounding up and down the floor. A buzzer rang, signaling the exchange of players.

Then it clicked. We had lived below in the basement. I was looking down into the stairwell where B and C and I'd passed so many evenings. Graffiti now covered the steps and the cement block walls. Names, a swastika, gang tags. I went down and tried to peer in the windows. Someone had added chain link over the glass to prevent break-ins. I could make out the room where we used to hold our volunteer meetings, only now it appeared to be a preschool. There were small chairs and tables and children's drawings on the walls.

I walked around to the front of the building. Several young white boys stood on the steps, and a heavy-set middle-aged man in a dirty white tee shirt stared out at the street. I went on in, thinking I should talk to someone but not sure how to explain my presence. The center seemed smaller, not nearly as imposing as it had years before. I avoided the basketball game and went on down the inside stairs, but the doors at the bottom were locked.

Back upstairs, I sauntered into the gym and watched the game for a moment. The players were intent and there was the happy din of competition. On the sidelines sat a no-nonsense young woman who seemed to be officiating. She wore torn jeans and a tee shirt, and her blonde hair was pulled back in a ponytail. She knew all the players by name and was yelling instructions. When I asked if she was in charge she nodded distractedly. I asked if there was any chance I could see the downstairs.

Without asking why, she grabbed a key, shouted to a couple of kids sitting with her, and escorted me down. I was relieved she didn't seem the least bit curious about why I was here. It was a question not easily answered.

"Here," she said unlocking the door, "just lock up when you leave."

She left me alone. I pushed the door open slowly and walked into the empty room. There was the faint smell of preschool: paste, small animals in cages, markers, children. I walked around and looked at the various children's projects in progress. It occurred to me then that the art work plastering the walls could well belong to the children of Junior and Richard—the next generation.

I walked back out and down the hall past the restrooms and the gang shower. A door to the right was open. A sign on it said "Office." The young woman from upstairs was now inside the shabby room engaged with two boys clearly solving some minor dispute. This was the room where the girl volunteers had slept that summer, where C and I had shoved our cots up close so we could whisper after the others had fallen asleep. Now it was a hodge podge of papers and junk and a couple of battered desks.

The young woman motioned me in, while the two boys scuffled playfully. She seemed absorbed and overburdened, but I took a chance. It turned out she was an Americorps volunteer, regretfully nearing the end of her two-year stint at the center. She loved her work and was going to miss the kids she'd gotten close to. She still hadn't asked who I was, and it occurred to me she might be assuming I had once been a child myself at this center.

So, I offered that I'd been an AFSC volunteer in the seventies, and she said, "What's that?" I could tell she was just being polite, so I kept things simple: "Another volunteer organization like yours. It was run by the Quakers."

120

"Never heard of it," she said.

At my request, she dug down in the drawer for some pamphlets on Americorps, but she wasn't having much luck finding them. I apologized for interrupting, and she assured me it was okay and continued to search.

"How's the neighborhood now?" I asked.

She shrugged. "Still poor white trash."

"Violence?"

"Sure," she said.

Several more children showed up, each needing permission or explanations. The volunteer turned her harried attention to them, and I realized there was no point in lingering. So Americorps had now replaced AFSC in a neighborhood that had not changed much in twenty years. And probably twenty years from now another frazzled and dedicated young woman, volunteering for the next organization to come along, would be leading the returning Americorps volunteer through the same center.

It is always odd to try to go back in time and track the past. I wanted some evidence that our three months had not been a waste. I had given my time that summer to children I would no longer recognize, but whose memories I carried with me. Overhead the basketball pounded across the court, followed by the thunder of feet. The Americorps volunteer glanced upwards, and I took my cue and left.

Just as the sun was setting, I took advantage of the last fifteen minutes of light to drive through the neighborhood I had once strolled with B and C. I decided to find Junior's house. It had been, I was sure, a white clapboard on a corner by itself, up on a slight rise, with a porch. I had a very strong image of Junior eagerly waiting out front, hair slicked down, for our center van to pick him up. In the yard, his brother in greasy overalls would be at work on a car. On the porch his pretty teenage sister would wait with her baby. She never spoke, but would always smile and wave exuberantly at C and me, as if we might have been friends under other circumstances.

Junior would be a grown man now, I thought. If he'd ever learned to read he might actually have avoided jail and found a decent job.

Driving by, I looked into the faces of the people standing around on their porches as if I'd find clues. I took in details: the explosion of yard art (black and white ceramic jockeys, whirligigs, ceramic geese in people clothes), children's toys scattered, the tattoos on a tough's arm, a couple of rough women smoking on a porch and eying the street. In one dirt yard in front of what appeared to be an abandoned house stood several young white adolescents in baggy pants. They had bandanas around their heads. They collectively gave my car a long, lingering glance, ever vigilant as to who was passing. The next house was brightly lit, front door and windows wide open. There were Catholic icons everywhere, images of Mary illuminated among numerous candles. It reminded me of a small chapel, or living rooms of houses in my old Latino neighborhood in San Francisco.

I looped up and down several different alleys; trash was heaped all around and spilling from broken garbage bags. A number of backyards were nothing more than hard dirt surrounded by chain-link fences. Over and over I saw "Beware of Dog" signs and "No Trespassing" notices.

Back on a narrow side street, a pickup cruised by with a Rottweiler in back barking its head off. The driver slowed down and stared, and I realized he had noticed the Calfornia license plate that is permanently affixed to the front of my old Toyota. In the twilight, several children in over-sized tee shirts clustered at someone's back door, and a distracted woman handed them out something. I read the bumper stickers off parked cars (Confederate flags and various refer-

121

ences to Jesus, along with gang graffiti). As more and more lights came on in windows, I slowed down trying to get glimpses inside. What exactly was I looking for? Evidence that somehow things were better, or worse? Evidence that I would find something familiar? Did I think I might actually recognize someone?

I learned in a recent call to the American Friends' Service Committee that volunteers in their summer work camps now mostly work overseas. "We haven't done that kind of inner-city work here in the U.S. for a long, long time," the person at the other end of the phone informed me. And I felt an odd pang for something lost.

The current AFSC materials floating around on the front seat of my car included an impressive list of what they had accomplished in the last year: "Sent school supplies to children in Haiti . . . Filed nearly two thousand applications for political asylum for Salvadorans in New Jersey, California, and Florida . . . Shipped more than twenty-two tons of clothing, sheets and towels, blankets, hand-knit items, yardage, and sewing supplies, and medical supplies to places all over the world . . . Rebuilt health clinics in earthquake-devastated Armenia."

On the back page of the Quaker Service Bulletin, a newsletter put out by the AFSC, my eye was attracted to the request for contributions. "Extending the Circle," said the caption heading the pink contributors' form. "I want to extend my circle of caring this holiday season with gifts to these areas," and then it listed several ways in which a monetary contribution might be used. These were the choices: Haiti/pig repopulation; New Mexico/rug weaving, water rights; Mozambique/women's development.

Before I got on Highway 37 heading back to Bloomington, I pulled into the crowded Village Pantry parking lot a couple blocks down from the Mary Rigg Center. Cars were pulling in and out. I sat for a moment, map in hand, trying to get my bearings. Two small blond boys, each carrying a plastic sack of groceries, exited the store and together took the shortcut through an adjacent trash-ridden lot in the dark. An impatient, tough-looking girl in tight jeans and cowboy boots, her middle exposed to show off her pierced navel, jumped out of a car and strode with the hyped-up, agitated pace of a crank addict, her face hard beyond her years. Next to me a couple argued in their car, windows rolled down, about whether the man should drive while drinking. The man snapped at the woman, started the engine, and backed out.

By now darkness had fallen and there was nothing left to see. Driving back to Bloomington, I struggled to remember the words of St. Paul in his Second Epistle to the Corinthians. When I got home, I had to look them up: "Though I speak with the tongues of men and of angels, and have not charity, I am become as sounding brass, or a tinkling bell. . . . Though I have all faith, so that I could remove mountains, and have not charity, I am nothing. And though I bestow all my goods to feed the poor, and though I give my body to be burned, and have not charity, it profiteth me nothing. Charity suffereth long and is kind; charity envieth not; charity vaunteth not itself, is not puffed up."

Who, I wondered, will step in at the Mary Rigg Center after the Americorps volunteer leaves?

122

CROSSED ROADS
(The Midwestern Covenant)
Andrew Levy

In his recent, Pulitzer Prize winning book, *God: A Biography*, Jack Miles presents an amended view of the covenant that God offers the Jewish people. The Bible, Miles suggests, depicts contracts offered between individuals (Moses, Abraham) and God, contracts that might be extended to the families of those individuals, but not explicitly to entire peoples. Specifically, he describes the song of thanks and triumph that a startled and grateful people offered God after He parted the Red Sea for them and drowned their enemies. Thank you for what you have done, the Jews told God, and for what you are about to do: slay the Philistines, Moabites, and Edomites for us, clear the land of Israel so that we may settle there, and come to live among us on a high throne in a high temple we will build for you. As Miles blandly notes, however, God has not offered to commit any of these actions. He has made broad promises to protect Moses, whom He seems to like, and protected Moses' people essentially because Moses seemed to like them.

Don't pretend you can part a body of water for a group of people and not expect them to make certain assumptions. Could it be that the status of the Jews as a chosen people was not endowed by God, but taken by the Jews themselves, squeezing themselves through a loophole in God's logic and claiming for themselves a story that would make sense of their suffering and allegiance to one another? And what would God do when, having offered Moses a special arrangement, and with stringent rules, he found instead an entire race of people, bedraggled but hopeful, sitting on his doorstep? Honor the contract, surely, but reinvent the terms; make being chosen a far more ironic reward than He originally intended? Or honor the contract, but with little enthusiasm, sensing perhaps (and perhaps rightly so) that, having chosen themselves, this people would make for themselves their own radical and complex destiny?

In a less credulous age, there would be a real jesuitical snideness to Miles' argument that the Jews were not chosen by God, but cajoled his serene Goodness into cohabitation and special consideration. In an age like ours, however, what emerges instead is a forthright parable of ethnicity in America, of what it means to be officially different from those around you. To be Jewish means belonging to an ethnicity defined by no biological code, no hue of skin or turn of eyelid (it takes one gaze upon the blonde and ginger mops that occupy the Kol Nidre service at any synagogue in Indianapolis or Louisville to realize how much distance lies between the Jewished stereotype of dark curly locks, oversized noses, and swarthy skin and the reality of assimilation and polyglot). A name can make no small marker, but can be erased by the coarse whim of an Ellis Island customs agent or, in more recent times, by 750 dollars and a visit to a lawyer who advertises on early morning television. In a real sense, one wakes up every morning and decides to be Jewish that day, for another day. One chooses to belong to a people that, as an act of faith (as opposed to an act of God, or an act of Congress), choose to unbelong.

At the same time, it is important to note that virtually no one who considers himself or herself Jewish (and this includes myself) actually believes this, regardless of the epistemological and spiritual possibilities such latitude might bring. To throw off one's Judaism in the morning feels no more possible than tossing off a tibia and a kneecap or two. There is almost no conviction in the argument that identity—specifically ethnic identity—is nothing more than performance and social construction, when the machinery of memory that makes nurture feel like nature is so mysterious and tenacious. It is for this reason that Judaism remains the court jester among the ethnic identities that occupy contemporary America. Lacking any biological code (or even the surfeit of codes, hybrids of codes, and shades of codes that provide the African-and Hispanic-American communities with their internal heterogeneity), the endurance of Judaism in the late-twentieth-century presents a constant reminder that ethnicity is nothing more than a cultural phenomena— a people telling God that they are different, or having other people tell God they are different. At the same time, it provides irrefutable evidence that the bond that attaches the American to his or her non-American ethnic antecedents remains intact and unintelligible— that God, or something that seems as opaque as the will of God, is telling you that you are not like everyone else.

Unfettered by any biological code, the Hebrew story of a chosen people and their relationship to the Lord could float free and abstract through centuries, mooring itself to any group that needed it and was willing to abide by its few strictures. This is the story of how Judaism came to America before the Jews of Europe and the Ural steppes ever treated America as anything more than a rumor among cousins. In the eighteenth and nineteenth centuries, American slaves would see Exodus in their dreams and sing it in their songs, and would see Moses in every leader who offered passage to the Canaan of the free North. In his legendary "Citie on the Hill" sermon on the Arbella ship in 1630, John Winthrop told his audience of 700 edgy Puritans that "the God of Israel"—no imitation, no ancestor, but the Biblical entity Himself—had made a special covenant with them, and would live among them when they reached Boston. He quoted Moses, quoted him again, and finished by quoting him at length, merging his voice indivisibly with that of the Biblical figure, merging the history of the Puritans of Massachusetts Bay indivisibly with that of the Hebrews. It would take that kind of commitment from God ("he hath given us leave to make our own articles," Winthrop tells his audience, reminiscent of the gap Miles finds in the Biblical story between God's intent and the Jewish interpretation of His intent) to clear wilderness like this. But having offered His commitment (or tacitly allowed the Puritans to believe that such a commitment was not unreasonable), God would ask something of these fledging Americans in return. He would make them retell the story of their exceptional status (that tenacious machinery of memory again) until the idea that America was a promised land and that Americans were a chosen people persisted even among generations who had long ceased to believe in God in any way that implied a contractual obligation to be good, or to send troops overseas to make others be good.

That is the official story of how Judaism came to America. Then there is the secret text, the apochrypha. There is Moses Levy, a sixteenth-century Moroccan aristocrat who bought land in Central Florida from the Spanish crown, convinced that other successful Jews from throughout Europe and Africa would want to retire there (Rule Number One of American Judaism: it is never too early to start buying real estate in Florida). And for every Moses, there are acolytes. There is Levy Andrew Levy (his name a playground singsong of my own, and vice versa), an eighteenth-century frontiersman and fur trader, Oxford-born, part-time political conspirator, one-time Indian captive (mistaken by Pontiac's soldiers as a member of a family of unscrupulous Canadian Levys), observant Jew, and one of the very first handful of men to leave Philadelphia (and all Philadelphia offered) to settle the territory of Indiana. Levy Andrew Levy, whose uncommon insistence on dealing face to face with the Iroquois nations compelled him in great sweeping circles across the Ohio Valley and headfirst into the mystery of the Midwest. Moses Levy, with dreams of condominiums and Orlando and Boca Raton so prescient that one can only wonder what other absurd details have taken purchase among the DNA. These Levys need not be remembered solely for the hard mercantile edge they doubtless possessed. We are here instead to consider the inchoate hopefulness and vision that their actions suggest, the quality of men and women whom three thousand years have trained to be rootless even amidst wealth and security, and in their rootlessness to possess an innate and unchartable sensitivity to the possibilities of a strange land and its people. But what if, in some odd Doppler effect of history, the residents of that strange land were dreaming that they were you before you ever really showed up? Would you be rooted more than you were prepared to endure, or dispossessed in a new way only the cagiest God could ever imagine?

There's the query. You know the saying: two Jews, three opinions. Here is my offering: one Jew, one American city (a clean, percolating crossroads, one that should do quite nicely for the inquiry), three opinions.

2

It is only by relative standards that Indianapolis is inhospitable to the Hebrew faith, a lonely place for the Jew. Roughly 10,000 Jews live in Indianapolis, or slightly more than one percent of the total population of the city. By comparison, slightly less than one percent of the population of Great Britain is Jewish. Slightly more than 10,000 Jews live in the entire country of Spain. There is no country in Eastern Europe where more than a few thousand Jews reside. But the Jewish population of the city of Philadelphia is thirty-five times larger than that of Indianapolis. And the Jewish population of New York City is six times larger than that of Philadelphia.

Since 1860, the Jewish population of Indianapolis (except for a brief period after World War I) has remained around one percent, a record of consistency and evenhandedness paradigmatic of the culture of the city but virtually unique nationwide. For decades, as Judith Endelman documents in *The Jewish Community of Indianapolis*, it was always aberrant, ambitious Jews who turned up here: German-born country peddlers in the 1850s, clothing merchants and tailors in the 1880s and 1890s, skilled laborers shipped here from the overcrowded Lower East Side of New York by relocation organizations in the 1900s and 1910s, a sudden influx of Sephardim, refugees from the Third Reich in the 1930s and again after the war, Soviet emigres in the early 1990s bursting through a porous Iron Curtain. Unlike the cities of the East, which experienced Jewish population booms and counter-reformations of anti-Semitism throughout the early part of the century, the Jewish and Protestant communities of Indianapolis absorbed their slender share of the Eastern European influx with comparative equanimity: a few more Gentile-only clubs, but no riots, and only the palest hues of job discrimination (try to find a Jewish plumber in this town). When the Ku Klux Klan took over the governor's office and the state house in 1924, the Jews of Indianapolis were cautious, but showed self-confidence uncharacteristic of diasporic communities: responding to a Klan "Buy American" campaign in 1925, Louis and Rose Shapiro actually changed the name of their American Grocery Store to Shapiro's and decorated its storefront with Jewish stars. Boondocked in a city that was more ethnically

125

diverse in 1860 than 1960, in the middle of a state that was ninety-five percent Protestant by 1920, the Jews of Indianapolis were never populous enough to intimidate the surrounding religious community, and were always just populous enough to cohere to one another. And so they advanced rapidly and advanced patiently, painstakingly assembling minyans, eradicating poverty on their own terms, working their way to the Northside, and always building a better synagogue.

I came to Indianapolis in 1992, having been raised in New York City, and educated in Philadelphia. By profession, and by inclination, I have spent much more time thinking about what it means to be American than I have thought about what it means to be Jewish. In Philadelphia, or New York, I could always let someone else be the Jew (there always seemed to be someone willing to do it), and I would gravitate toward the safe center, immerse myself in knowing and taking at least scholarly possession of a country that seemed explicitly to belong to others. In Indianapolis, however, everything changed. In an early visit to Shapiro's defiant deli, I found myself sitting beside a group of elderly men discussing the Ku Klux Klan with a degree of openness and intimacy that would have appalled me anywhere, but was absolutely disorienting in a place whose broad popularity certainly seemed to represent acceptance of Jewish culture here (later I would come to realize that their public discussion in fact represented just such acceptance, albeit on the midwestern terms of the covenant). Men and women at work introduced themselves to me, and gave me advice about which supermarkets carried kosher products, or the location of a synagogue—assuming, in a manner alien to the cities of the East Coast, that being Jewish meant a single unyielding set of customs. Students—sometimes students I had never met—began asking me questions about Judaism, assuming my expertise on its esoterica. Lastly, my

surname (the Jewish equivalent of "Smith," and another crucial symbolic marker of acceptance) became a site of contestation, mispronounced, mispelled, or a subject for conversation, a constant reminder that I was different, and that the people here maintained control of my difference. In Indianapolis, I discovered, there was all the America a man could ever need. But I had become one of only a few Jews in the metaphorical room, and everyone one else seemed to know it before I did. I had entered history.

Unaffiliated and diffidently observant, I am still a newcomer here, no spokesman for any experience but my own. Since moving to Indianapolis, I have discovered the freak of opportunity that allowed me to spend my entire life until this point within two of the few cities in world history where a Jew need not feel like an outsider. In Indianapolis, I discovered the diaspora, and a sense of exile. But I also discovered a sense of tradition, which is to say that I met my ancestors for the first time. I am the country peddler come west on horseback. Or that cabinetmaker relocated to the Midwest in 1912 because the cosmopolitan cities of the East had all the cabinetmakers they needed. I can see them, or an exemplary one of them, satchel in hand, waiting for a friend of a friend of a relative, squinting upward at the front of Union Station, then turning to look at the uncomplicated and overwhelming Indiana sky, and the spiritual monochromacity of the life that bustled serenely underneath it, along Meridian, Washington, and Market. A Protestant sky, my exemplary cabinetmaker says to himself. How did they make the sky Protestant?

3

One third of the state's population can claim German descent. For periods during the nineteenth century, three out of every four foreign-born men and women settling in Indianapolis had emigrated from Germany. And they left their mark throughout the city: in the surnames of Indianapolis's favorite sons and daughters (Vonnegut and Lugar), in the public buildings (now landmarks) designed by a distinguished series of German-born architects, among the legendary social clubs (the Turnverein and the Athenaeum) that remain standing, and most memorably among the genetic stock, in the cornsilk hair and windex eyes of Dan Quayle and several million other succinctly Aryan Hoosiers.

To the modern Jew, the memory of the Holocaust produces an almost instinctive distrust of any show of German nationality and culture, an unkindly but inevitable mindset where history dictates that one nation cannot help seeing the powder keg in another. But Indianapolis plays tricks with this distrust. The German men and women who came to Indiana themselves sought escape from religious and economic repression in Europe, and the facsimiles of German culture that they generated in these midwestern flatlands wore the mark of diaspora as strongly as did any synagogue, bearing nostalgia for a homeland detached from affection for its churches and government. In larger part, however, explanation can be found in the torpid demographics of twentieth-century Indiana, when the emigration of foreign nationals into the state slowed to a pace far below that of neighboring states. Just as the Jewish community of contemporary Indianapolis is almost uniquely marked by its continuity with its nineteenth-century antecedents, the German cultural presence in the city also bears the contours of the nineteenth-century homeland, of beergardens and gothic cathedrals and a quaint pre-industrial efficiency. One begins to feel that the Jews and Gentiles of modern Indianapolis have reproduced (or kept alive, as in a hothouse) some rough equivalent of the relationship between those two groups that existed one hundred years ago, as if the land, architecture, and genetic stock of this place were designed to remind you that

history never happened here, that death camps and blood libels still belonged to an unthinkable future, not an unspeakable past.

Unfortunately, there still remains the matter of the powder keg. Anti-Semitism has made history riotous because it lacks consistency, moving against the available Jews in dim algebrae of love and hate when the wrong people rise and the wrong people fall. The more Indianapolis reminds its diasporic visitor of the Germany that preceded the Germany we all regret, the more one wonders what might lie dormant here and, more broadly, what causes a tolerant community to pin the tail on its scapegoats. It is not as if Indiana lacks its own powder kegs that it needs to borrow others from this rich but exclusively metaphorical association with the blood sins of other countries. But it is only from this perspective that Indianapolis becomes precious and complete. This city prides itself on its sins and virtues of domesticity, and honors its children and its veterans with every available symbol. It requires a reminder that the leaf-strewn streets of the Northside, the Appalachian labyrinths of the Southside, and the shimmering malls of downtown and uptown all contain the possibility of tragedy, and the seed of anarchy.

This is the inverse but forceful logic of the Kaddish, the Jewish prayer that contains within its words so much gratitude for life that it has become the customary prayer of mourning. Its words can be said in service only by those individuals who have recently lost a loved one, as if only those individuals could truly understand the sacredness of life with any real immediacy or urgency. Turn the Kaddish into a law of geography: understand a place better because the Chamber of Commerce visions of its durability, thrift, and order don't tell you anything about the civil war that lies waiting in an idle gaze. Love a dangerous country more than a safe one.

127

4

After living in Indianapolis for a few months, I found that an item I possessed needed repair, and so I availed myself of the services of a downtown merchant. I will keep the merchant's name (and his occupation) anonymous here, not because he did anything criminal, or even faintly compromising, but because anonymity appeared to be one of the codicils implicit in our conversation, and in his relationship to the city at large. He was beyond retirement age—the combined lifespans of himself and his father would reach back to that seminal wave of Jewish immigration to Indianapolis—and he was particularly conscious of mortality and of history. In his will, he wanted to endow a chair in Judaic Studies to the local university that had offered the most sympathy to Judaism and to Jewish causes during his lifetime. I offered my own school, but he rejected politely. I offered another, but he rejected it as well. Before my item was repaired and my bill was paid, he had rejected the name of every university within a fifty-mile radius of his shop, and with every rejection he grew more convinced that he wanted to endow that chair.

Three years later, I was sitting in a Broad Ripple bar, drinking beer with a graduate student, and listened while he described the house he was sharing with other graduate students. It had belonged to a local businessman who had recently died. His heirs had little interest in his house or its contents, and left it roughly furnished for prospective tenants. When the graduate student had answered the advertisement, he was shown a study that was filled with fifty years worth of Judaica—religious pieces, books, photographs, and letters and commemorative items evidencing a strenuous if distanced attachment to the State of Israel. The graduate student was invited to throw out the contents of the study, and make it his bedroom. He rented the room, and moved its contents to the basement.

At this point I asked the name of the businessman who had owned the house, and for some less obvious reason I paid no attention to the answer. Since moving to Indianapolis, I have met a fair number of its Jewish residents. I am half in love with them, with the absence of friction that at least appears to mark their daily lives in a Gentile society. I adore the sight (and I am aware of the voyeuristic quality of this adoration) of the Orthodox passing along suburban lawns in grey dusk on their way to Shabbat services. I adore no less the Conservative and Reformed with whom I have fallen in and out and in again: the doctor and his working wife, the boyish newspaper editor, the communitarian women, the blind dates (courtesy of the communitarian women), the new emigre, the Rabbi, a second Rabbi. But the man to whose shop I brought my broken item was singular among these Jews, for only he appeared to sense that there existed some tragedy in assimilation, and some tragedy in the failure to assimilate, and that no one knew which form of alienation was worth the greater aversion. Sitting on that Broad Ripple bar stool, I had no desire to discover that the expansive dream of the downtown merchant to make Judaism manifest to Indiana with a shining endowed chair had produced nothing else than the extraordinary introversion of a single room full of Judiaca in a handsome house on the Northside. It was better that they be remembered as two different men, two different sides to the same destiny.

Or better: two different men approaching each other at a crossroads, their possessions and their secrets on their backs, under a timeless sun. The history of the Jews in the twentieth century (at least, in American eyes) has been perceived as such an urban phenomenon (the Lower East Side of New York City, the ghettoes of Warsaw and Lodz) that it is easy to forget how Judaism was born in the desert among farmers, nomads, and shepherds, and how well it thrived among farms and at the markets of numberless vast civilizations. But the resurrection of Israel is only the most startling reminder that Judaism was first a religion of sand and blue sky, and only latterly a culture of the asphalt. We should not be surprised to find how well Judaism suits Sunbelt cities such as Phoenix or Las Vegas, where the ancient legacy of a desert people outlasts and eventually effaces the far younger and more callow alienation of American Jews from the Sunbelt consensus of conservative politics, a Gentile God, and a frozen supermarket bagel. And we should be even less surprised at how Judaism thrives in Indianapolis, which has never had a truer self than its translucent crossroads self, a place to bring your wares to market and to leave part of yourself behind—a little Seattle in Broad Ripple, a little Belfast in Rocky Ripple, a little Copenhagen on South Meridian, a little Brooklyn and a little Haifa in Nora, Carmel, Lockerbie. It is not likely that every Jewish household in Indianapolis contains one room devoted to its Judaica, but what a fine symbol that room makes for the soul within every Jew that resides metaphorically in Jerusalem, and in so doing remains unassimilated to the home that claims the diasporic soul, and the body that bears them both. It is not at all difficult to imagine the entire city laden with these odd, quiet rooms, guarding the core values of all the ethnicities, religions, sexual choices, and eccentricities of heart that must be made subterranean to produce a place as superficially placid as this one. Every culture, minor or major, gets to tell its own story sooner or later. Diasporic cultures learn to wait their turn. You only need to see one room full of objects dedicated to a hidden devotion—you only need to imagine such a room—to realize what a miraculous secret life a city like Indianapolis must possess, inevitably possess.

129

ICONOGRAPHY:
Scenes of Indianapolis and Elsewhere
Michael Martone

Indianapolis

It is midnight. On the front lawn of the church we surround the *Kouvouklion*, the small decorated wooden table with a little dome used as a catafalque to transport the *Epitafios*, a painted cloth icon representing Christ entombed. It is midnight, and the bells of Holy Trinity begin to peal, starting in sets of three, as sets of three are an important part of the ritual of Orthodox faith, perhaps even more so at a church named for the Holy Trinity. The bells ring, first in threes, then exploding into ever expanding multiples, creating rippling patterns of pitch and timbre with no melody so that there is no notion of when, or if, the now cacophonous pealing will end. At the same time, Father Gounaris begins the triumphant chant, *Christos Anesti*, Christ has risen. The congregation sings with the singing priest, the lit candles we hold inscribing the sign of the cross in the air before us, a kind of musical conducting, sweeping up then right, then left while the bells boom and the chant hits its heavy solid beats.

I am standing with my back to North Pennsylvania Street, looking back through the dome of the *Kouvouklion*, facing Father Gounaris who now begins the chant again in English:

> Christ has risen
> from the dead
> by trampling down
> death by death…

Holy Trinity Church is behind him, and my eyes follow the swing of the *Pascha* candles upward to the blue black sky studded with stars over Indianapolis of all places. Indianapolis, whose name is a fossilized amalgam of languages and histories, misidentifications by emigrants of one people from one place with another people in another place and its epithet of fragmentary Greek, *polis*, the city, yes, but also the people in Greek, the same Greek that is now again, as the song returns to Greek, in the air over this city and these people.

On either side of the open church doors, dogwood trees are just beginning to bloom. My response to seeing the pale white buds at this moment—with the bells, the singing, the candles—is complex. At first I am surprised as I had heard from a friend here in Indianapolis that the dogwoods and red buds were blighted this year, dying without blooming. She had told me this as I made plans for coming up from Alabama, where I live now, to this Easter service in Indianapolis. At the time I talked to her, the dogwoods and red buds, ten hours further south and a month before, were glorious in color. I had just moved to the South and had never seen such a spring. I grew up in Indiana, in Fort Wayne, where it was a rare spring when my grandfather, who moved from Kentucky to Fort Wayne, actually was able to coax the flowering trees into flower. It was my grandfather who always repeated each spring the legend that the wood for the cross was taken from the dogwood, that Judas hanged himself on the red bud, its crimson flower representing drops of blood.

So my discovery of the blooming dogwoods at the doorway of

the church made me think of all these things, the coincidence of many narratives, and how symbols and stories are transported as people move around in the world. To me the dogwood and the red buds always seemed like southern trees, Kentucky trees, but in all those years of my grandfather's retelling I never thought until this moment that the dogwood and the red buds might not be Mediterranean trees. Are they even native in the Holy Land? And I am thinking about the nature of the relationship of how people and what they believe are connected to the places they left and those they inhabit now. And I am thinking this on the front lawn of a Greek church a couple of blocks from 38th Street in Indianapolis where my grandfather, joking, always insisted the South began. And on this spot, and in a foreign language, I am listening to a very old story about death being dead and thinking of my grandfather who died in the same year the dogwoods were supposed to never bloom in Indiana but did.

Sparta

I wake up, and I am in Indiana again. I see, through the windows of the bus, fields of elephant eye high corn. How strange! When I fell asleep I was touring the Peloponese in Greece, riding a bus up from the ruined city of Monemvasia to Sparta. I fell asleep in the semi-arid rocky landscape to which I'd grown accustomed. Orange and olive groves, date palms and fig trees. Now this. How un-Greece like! Rows of green tasselled corn and red tractors, pre-fab metal buildings and spinning windmills. Sparta itself looks like no other Greek city I have ever seen. It is platted out on a grid like many a small town in the American Midwest, not the viney, over-lapping lattice growth of the typical Greek city or village whose design reaches back to the ancient memory of the Minotaur's maze on Crete and the warrens of alleyways and paths

that acted as defenses against pirate attacks on the dice-white island villages spilling off mountains down to the sea. Sparta, then, is an anomaly. Built by the philhellene French in the nineteenth century on the site of the militaristic city-state of classical Greece, restored not to its former glory, as no one remembered what it had looked like when the Romans leveled it and salted the earth, but to the specs of enlightened empire design. So present day Sparta, like Indianapolis, say, is an imaginary city, one staked-out and planned by fiat, not organically evolved from continuous inhabitation. This Sparta appeared overnight. And it made its appearance about the same time the American Midwest was sprouting towns. So it recreates, in my mind, this strange association of the feel of its streets and spaces.

Consequently, Sparta isn't on the usual must see lists. But I'm not on the usual tour. A few years before this trip, I married a Greek-American woman, Theresa, from Baltimore, and introduced her to Indiana by taking her on an extensive car trip of the state soon after we met. I like to say, half jokingly, that we honeymooned in Indiana. We stopped in Santa Claus and French Lick. We visited the almost empty convent in Ferdinand where the nuns showed us the vestments they had made and the tea towels embroidered with the state bird. At Columbus, we walked among the architectural monuments and discovered across from the Barthelomew County Courthouse the turn-of-the-century soda fountain, Zaharikos, run by a Greek family. Were they from Sparta? No, perhaps that was the soda fountain in Princeton, Indiana, or the candy shop in Iowa Falls, Iowa. No it was the one in Wilton, Iowa, the Wilton Candy Kitchen. Or it was somewhere else in the Midwest—a coffee shop, a pizza take-out, a bar and grill—where the proprietor had a picture on the wall of Mount Tayegetos looming over Sparta, and I told him of our trip there.

131

This trip to Greece is Theresa's returned favor for my hustling her around Indiana. It has been cobbled together wonderfully by local bus and her agency with the language. We visit the comparable off-the-beaten-track, roadside attractions of rural southern Greece. Here, in Sparta, we stumble upon this strange intersection with my home and homeland. During that late evening's *volta*, the nightly walk Greeks take before retiring, we sort out what remains in a place to create Place and what remains in our memories to create who we are. And call to mind what it is we take with us when we move from place to place as we move along amidst the Spartans, strolling, heading toward the well-lit *Zaharoplasteion* on the square for *pagato* which you and I know as ice cream.

Indianapolis

Almost midnight and all the lights of Holy Trinity Church are being extinguished. The Orthodox service is designed as a drama with its recreation weekly of the Last Supper, the Crucifixion, and the resurrection. The Church, I think, is very good at creating moving stage pictures out of very simple elements—light and shadow, bread and wine and water and oil, the few gestures of the priest.

My sons were both baptized in Greek churches, Sam at Saint Nicholas in Baltimore and Nick at Saint Sophia in Syracuse, New York. The baptism is a good example of what I mean. The babies, naked, were dunked, totally immersed, three times, of course, in the name of the Father, the Son, and the Holy Spirit, into the water of the font which had been anointed on its surface at the start with a cross of floating olive oil. At last, howling, the babies were hauled aloft by the priests. They were red, wet, dripping, oily, bawling, exactly, exactly the way they looked when they were born physically a few months before this second birth. And seeing them then, again, fierce, heaving for breath, alive, I was again at their first

births and all my visceral responses kicked in once more. And that is the point—that this new birth is not just like birth, it is birth.

On *Pascha*, Easter, the weekly symbolic evocations of sacrifice and resurrection are themselves transformed, taken to an even higher intensity. Now, in this dark, the iconostasis, the screen that separates the nave of the church from the sanctuary, takes on a heavier weight of darkness, the wall of the tomb. Suddenly, a single candle flame erupts behind the Beautiful Gate, the center doorway of the iconostasis, backlighting the grill work of the gate and defining its bulk. Its piercing rays seem to outline us all in the darkness of the church. With just this single light we can make out, barely, the gate being slowly opened, the stone being rolled away, the light moving toward us. And then the flame splits into two lights and then almost instantly doubles in number again and then again, moving in quick leaps left and right, streaming now from person to person back toward me in the last row to the candle I hold.

Oh, I suppose a part of me, the modern man, two thousand years after the stone was rolled away and the Light of the World appeared, sees through this ritual or, more exactly, sees it as only symbolic. That is, I could engage in it on this intellectual level, from a distance, for what it symbolizes, what it represents. The Church is the mother lode of symbols and metaphors. Everything teaches, everything represents something, everything prompts us to call to mind another time and place when the Son of God walked on Earth, when the Saints and Martyrs evangelized and died, when the heaven will be visited on earth. I understand all that because I am a user of metaphor myself. But at certain moments I forget to think and begin to feel. The metaphoric contraption works and, working, falls away, and I have been transported to these other places and times, transported into these stories and they are no longer merely stories. The Greek Church is very good at the manipulation of my senses into believing. And I do appreciate its skill as I am professionally a story teller, a writer of fiction and drama. But, at times, I even forget to remember to note my professional self-conscious respect and admiration, I forget to remember where I am really, in Indianapolis, in Indiana, and I am at the mouth of a tomb and I hear a voice saying: "The one you are looking for is not here."

Mystras

Outside Sparta is the ruined city of Mystras, one of the important Byzantine cities along with Monemvasia and Constantinople. It is a red brick ruin of the more recent Christian era so does not enjoy the tourist trade afforded the white marble ruins of the classical age. Theresa and I, it seems, have the place to ourselves. We wander through the acres of collapse, the piles of rubble marking the collapse of Greece into the Ottoman Empire six hundred years ago. There is, to our surprise, a working convent here. We peer through the grill of the gate and see a nun slowly sweep the flagstones of the courtyard. Surrounding the walled convent are huge piles of stone and dust, houses and shops and churches swept into huge heaps. Slowly a few of Mystras's churches have been rebuilt by donations from private citizens, some having their interior frescoes and icons restored to their medieval splendor. There is a tiny domed Saint Michael. We stumble upon a church named for the Virgin built into the side of the mountain. There is a guard inside who is happy to see us. He warns Theresa against taking photos of the *Pantocrator* or the *Theodoxos*, frescoes of Jesus the Ruler of the Universe and Mary the Mother of God, but then he turns away his hands entwined with *komboloi*, worry beads he worries, I suppose, on his lonely post, and with his back turned indicates with a little flick of his fingers to go ahead and take a picture. "See," the gesture says, "I am not looking." Theresa does put her

camera to her eye to focus on the Mother of God but discovers that it is too dark. Instead we stand in silence, our eyes sweeping over the walls and roof of the church, every inch of it decorated with paintings, paintings telling stories. Spontaneously, the guard starts singing, the monotonic a cappella chant of church, something from the vespers probably, perhaps just to demonstrate the acoustics of the mortar and stone but maybe because he wants to share this place with us, animate it fully so that we, in the few moments we visit, get a sense of his daily experience, a space brought back to life, in focus and in full voice.

Ames, Athens, Indianapolis

It is probably clear by now that I have lived in many places. I teach at universities so I have moved from Maryland to Iowa to Massachusetts to New York to Alabama. Perhaps, because I have moved so much, I tend to write about Indiana though I haven't lived there for years, a compensation for all my wandering. America, a nation of immigrants, has never had its own major outpouring of citizens. Its emigrations have all been internal—the farm to the city, the city to the suburb, the east to the west, the south to the north and back again. It is a great drama, community and claustrophobia on the one hand, freedom and rootlessness on the other—my one grandfather moving north out of Kentucky hauling its flora with him, my other grandfather leaving Italy and landing on Brandruff Street in Fort Wayne, Indiana, never to move again.

It is my story, of course, but America's story as well. The Greek Church's diaspora went along with the Greek people. It began from a very specific place called Greece, and its history intensely dramatizes the dilemma of identity and assimilation. How can a faith so rooted in a place make a place for itself elsewhere? Perhaps more than any other transplanted Christian faith, Greek

133

Orthodoxy suffers the question profoundly what with its national boundaries nearly indistinguishable with those of the church and the language. There is, moreover, the pride of that place and all that history. The Greeks, you recall, invented hubris. Paul, using the Greek language, proselytized, the word itself Greek, in the Athenian agora within living memory of Christ's life. The Church in tending the faith during the period of Ottoman hegemony did so by kindling the language and the ethnic identity. To be Greek and Greek Orthodox often seems seamless.

A funny story, probably apocryphal. We heard it from the Greek students we met when we moved to Ames, Iowa, and Iowa State University. The fraternities there were having a huge party advertised for Greeks only. It seems a Greek student, Yanni, showed up at the gate and was told he can't come in. "For Greeks only," the frat brothers say. "But I am Greek!" Yanni says. "No you're not Greek," he's told again. "I am Greek!" Yanni says, knowing it is enough just to assert this obvious truth. The Greek students telling us this story have in their telling a kind of poignancy, a sympathetic understanding of Yanni, their protagonist (a Greek word) and his inability to comprehend a Greek world not his own.

Tonight, in Indianapolis, I am Greek and I am not Greek. At the meal following the *Pascha* service I sit with five others, strangers to me until now. We introduce ourselves by playing the egg breaking game. Earlier, we were all given the red dyed Easter eggs as we filed out of church and into this very Hoosier gymnasium at the back of Holy Trinity to break the fast with a supper of lamb and feta and olives and christopsomi, the special Easter bread. We say *Christos Anesti* and tap the eggs' ends together, a kind of wishbone breaking contest. Mine survived all challenges. The woman next to me has just converted, having married, recently, the man next to

her. Her husband emigrated from Salonika as a young man. Christos Anesti, I say. Truly, he has risen, she says in English. Her husband is talking to his friend and his friend's wife in Greek. Something about a trick the one has played on the other convincing him that the candles this year would be replaced by flashlights. I believed him, he says, in English, laughing. This evening, Father had warned communicants to watch their candles so as not to set anyone's hair on fire. It made sense he says still laughing. The other man is Greek and doesn't speak English. He is visiting, like me. I want to ask him but can't because of the language how different this night is from Easter back home.

We represent all the variations of this faith, I think. I tell everyone I have come from Alabama. It is three o'clock Easter morning. I feel at home but also far away from home.

The Meteora

It is as if we are on the moon. On all sides, gigantic boulders, bleached by the sun and sanded smooth by the eons of rain and wind. It is a landscape like no other I have ever seen save maybe that of the background of a Roadrunner cartoon, naked buttes and precariously balanced rocks leering over sheer cliffs with massive crags. We are walking through this valley hedged around by one-piece mountains whose name, Meteora, suggests their arrival, whole, from heaven above.

Perched on the top tip of the largest boulders are the monasteries. Only recently has the bishop here ordered the cutting in of stairs to reach them. They still have the woven baskets, lowered from the trap doors of overhanging wooden wings of the houses to the valley floor. The monks still winch up water and food and more wood and stone to continue the impossible, asymmetrical building above.

We climb the sets of thousands of stairs to see the churches

134

and the icons, the frescoes in the rectories and the relics of the saints. On the way up we see a hermit's cave or two bored into the mountain face across the valley, a sheet of solid rock stained like a natural fresco with its own aesthetic nuance. At the top we are greeted by the monks as xenia—strangers, guests, pilgrims—and offered the traditional Greek hospitality of coffee and glika, incredibly sweet preserves of oranges, cherries, or grapes.

In one monastery, teetering above the toy city of Kalambaka below, a young monk with Coke-bottle-bottom lenses in his eyeglasses breathlessly relates to us the wonders of his recent trip to New York, *Nea Yorki*, and the results of laser surgery there. He recalls the shadows of the tall buildings, the canyons he walked through, the observation decks of skyscrapers. All around us are the ancient painted icons with their staring eyes and the open windows of the monastery looking out on the deep blue bottomless sky.

Des Moines, Cambridge, Indianapolis

I remember. "Signomi, Yiayia!" Excuse me, Grandmother. An usher says this at Saint George's in Des Moines as he slides the delicate old woman down along the slick pew so that others could pack in for the service.

I remember. A teenage girl in the narthex of the Saints Constantine and Helen in Cambridge whispers to her friend, "Aphrodite, let me use your hair brush" with a Boston accent.

It is hard to capture, perhaps, all that goes on during any one service. I am always taken by the juxtaposition of extreme solemnity of ritual with casual hubbub of earthbound life. As I watch, the priest and deacon and the altar boys scurry around and about the raised area in the front of the nave emerging from the sanctuary behind the iconastasis. They disappear and reappear at the north or south gates, move about sacred objects spontaneously, bustling like a janitorial crew. You see them dress and redress preparing for the great processions while all the time the chanters and choir can be singing like angels about the angels. Ushers hustle candles to the front, in ones or twos, brought to the fore to be placed beneath the various icons while latecomers light slim tapers in the open narthex in the rear of the church. The service is meant to be a dramatic recreation of the life and death of Christ, but as a play, it is most like the self-conscious kind, *Our Town*, say, with the stage manager stopping to comment on the action and move about stage property, set the scene to come. And just now Father Gounaris does break character and directs the congregation to watch out for the candle flame when taking communion. Earlier on the front lawn of Holy Trinity I watched as he nudged a new battery into the hand-held mic moments before the bells began to ring beatifically. It is like watching baseball, I think, the only sport where the ball doesn't do the scoring. You must watch the ball and the runners running, a wide view of the field. It is as much about the periphery as it is the pinpoint The Greek church is simultaneously homely and divine, human and ethereal. The priest is chanting within the sanctuary. We see him framed by the open portal of the Royal Gate. The choir singing something else. The evening ebbs and flows. The priest is an actor and then acts as a commentator or critic of the action, explains what has happened before our eyes, what is yet to come. Suddenly we are transfixed by the great procession of the Gospel or the Gifts; the parades of transfigurations, both miraculous and routine, parade before us.

There is much anxiety surrounding the veneration of icons in the church. Church literature is at pains to explain the difference between worship and veneration, how our love is directed to the one represented and not toward the material thing of wood and paint itself. It is clear to me that the icons are windows, a kind of porous

135

membrane separating these worlds, the corporeal and the spirit. While the liturgy is performed, both worlds are present, these overlapping spheres of space and place, the divine and human. I attend, at the same time, all the gestures and the words, sense the music and the incense. I wait and witness the tedium of certain parts while I am transfixed by other parts. I sense the capillary attraction between these realms. The evening contains and dramatizes all of these places and creates the possibility of imagining a wholly other dimension while being deeply rooted in our own mundane one.

Indianapolis

After the supper, early in the morning, I make my way through the crowded gymnasium over to Father Gounaris to thank him for this evening. I explain to him how I got here, here to Holy Trinity, to Indianapolis, this night. How my wife is Greek from Baltimore, *Valtimori* I say. "You say that really well," Father Gounaris compliments me. I give him a thumbnail of my wandering—the churches I know in Des Moines, Cambridge, Syracuse, Birmingham. I tell him of my sons' baptisms, my trips to Greece.

My whole life in a few quick gestures, blurring. I tell him what has interested me most is this dilemma of place and movement, how the Greek church is and is not Greek. At the end of the *Pascha* service, right before the eggs and the icon cards were distributed, before we sat down to dinner, Father Gounaris stepped forward, slightly winded from the long night's festivities but jazzed and obviously joyful, to address his flock. This impromptu homily touched on this very issue. He annunciated to the assembled flock what was obvious to us all, how different we all were from one another and how all bound up together we were now in one place and time. At Holy Trinity that night there were the sons and daughters of Greeks who would never set foot in Greece, there were converts converted for all reasons, and there were Eritreans from Africa in their native dress, there were descendants of Serbs, Russians, Poles, Macedonians, as well as Greek Americans who left their homeland for who knows what reasons and found themselves here. It was a prayer answered I thought, Father Gounaris recognizing the fact of our different story lines and their intersection here this night. He acknowledged this fact of faith in a few words of English, a language that will do as good as any.

136

Counting Losses
Aron Aji

I

Grapes under feet that crush them
turn whichever way they are turned.
You ask why I turn around you?
Not around you, I turn around myself.
— *Rumi*

The first time I was lost in Indianapolis, the dome of the mosque on Cold Spring Road was a sight as strange as reassuring. When I pulled in to the gas station to ask for directions, the attendant noticed my accent and said, "The mosque? Want the mosque?" pointing to the red-brick building still under construction at the time. "No, not the mosque, I need directions to I-65," I said, and perhaps because a lost man's only certainty is who he thinks he is, I added, "I am Jewish. I come from Turkey. I'm a Jew from Turkey." Visibly perplexed by the string of details, the attendant chose the one he could handle and gave me directions to the highway.

Seven months later, my wife, Joyce, and I would find ourselves in the same neighborhood, at the same gas station, this time asking for directions to the house we were scheduled to look at, the one we would end up buying. A house located within shouting distance from one of the very few mosques in North America, 9,000 miles away from my native city of hundreds of mosques and minarets.

II

With no thought of return, I still keep a set of keys to my family's home in Turkey, in remembrance of my grandmother's tin-box full of keys. As a child, I often took the tin-box from her armoire and secretly played with these long keys, short keys, flat, slender, black and silver keys, little aware of what I know now: that, in their mute way, they charted out for me the path back, the journey through transient houses, streets, villages, through countries and continents. In 1492, the Jews of Cordoba, Toledo, and Seville had taken their house keys with them to the Ottoman territories, expecting they would return to Spain. While in the new land, they kept adding keys to their boxes, each time they were forced to relocate in order to balance the minority populations in newly conquered cities. In her own lifetime, my grandmother added four keys to the endless chain. The ritual of keys is in response to the untenable present, a prayer uttered in quicksand.

III

The mosque on Cold Spring Road appears to sit awkwardly between its neighbors. The mosque's stately gate is on the back and none of its walls faces the road; instead one of its corners extends pointedly toward the road so that its niche to which the faithful turn in prayer faces Mecca.

Inside the synagogue, I mimic the congregants and turn toward Jerusalem. At wedding ceremonies, the bridegroom breaks a glass, punctuating the joyful occasion with solemnity, "If I forget thee, oh Jerusalem . . . ."

From Indianapolis, the distance between Jerusalem and Mecca is less than an inch, an almost unnoticeable shift of acquiescent feet on the perfect map of faith.

IV

The tin-box was one of the casualties of my grandparents' last move from one neighborhood to another, supervised by my mother who was sure we would move to Israel soon and believed that a fresh start should not be weighed down by the past. At nine, I sat with my family around a table for weekly Hebrew lessons. On my one and only visit to Israel in 1969, I could speak the language fluently enough to find my way around, to buy hot dogs and steak-a-la-pita, and to write a small prayer on the piece of paper which I put inside a crack on the Wailing Wall. Perhaps wanting to leave as little to chance as she could, mother dictated our prayers for a permanent return.

My mother grew up in the early years of the great exodus to the state of Israel. In the decades which spanned from her youth to my childhood, our community was practically emptied, shrinking from 30,000 to 4,000. Until the forties, Izmir housed small Jewish merchants of all trades. In my childhood during the sixties, only two vendors paid home visits. There were also five Jewish beggars, one for each week day, some of whom must have saved enough money to move to Israel. With these small people who had spun a precious web from house to house, our language, Ladino, also left us. Throughout these years, our mothers made several trips to Israel, diligently avoided any commitments which could not be easily broken, and taught themselves languages to read the literature necessary to prepare for the final move. And many left.

But mother remained. I am sure she could give many reasons why she remained. Yet, as I sit here in Indianapolis, having

so little desire to leave after years of departures, I am beginning to think that there is a kind of exhaustion which passes from mother to child, a fatigue which builds throughout uncertain arrivals, and which overwhelms the mind with the memory of a thousand metal keys.

V

Nazım Hikmet writes in one of his later poems: "Two things are forgotten only with death / the face of our mothers and the face of our cities." This, after years of unjust incarceration in his 'city' and restless wondering as a result of being expelled from his native land. One remembers what one can hold onto. If not reality, then its memory. Nazım's is an impossible courage to write, to withstand the stubborn dissapearance of past, to mend longing with memory: a spirituality of loss arrested by things remembered.

VI

Mohammed appeared in our street, on a vacant summer afternoon. Seeing us, he hastened his pace. Glenn straightened himself in his chair, when the large bearded man in long striped robe and sandals climbed the stairs to his porch. I watched. Arms and hands started flailing about, heads nodding yes and no. Soon, Glenn went inside the house, brought him a glass of lemonade. The man remained staring at his glass; he was clearly famished but wasn't drinking. Glenn came over and said to me, "He is looking for a home. He keeps saying 'khom.' He showed me in his dictionary. Want to come and help us out?"

I greeted the man in Arabic, "Salamun aleiqum," a phrase common to his and my native tongues. Heartily shaking my hand, he asked, "Muslim? Muslim?" pointing his finger at me then at Glenn. Replicating his gestures, I replied, "Yahoudi.

Hristian... Musa. Isa." I could tell he was disappointed. "Limonata," I said, pointing at the full glass, then making the gesture of drinking. He still wouldn't touch the glass. I presumed, correctly it turned out, that he wasn't sure if the drink was "clean" of alcohol. I tried to convince him by showing the word in his dictionary, but he remained hesitant. Then an idea came to me. I took the glass, held his hand and pulled him up. "Come," I gestured. He followed me to our house.

Inside, I showed him the Turkish ceramic plate hanging on our wall. On it was the opening sura of the Qur'an, inscribed in beautiful calligraphy. Then I gave him the glass. He smiled and drank and drank.

Mohammed was a merchant from Saudi Arabia. He and his father sold loudspeakers and Qur'an tapes to mosques throughout the Middle East. He came to the U.S. to learn English; he chose Marian College's ESL program because one of the brochures included a photo and a few lines of description of the mosque on Cold Spring Road. On the day he wandered into our neigborhood, he was looking for a room to rent in one of the houses he presumed were owned by Muslim families living around the mosque.

The following week, Mohammed visited our house daily. Then came along his brother, then his Saudi, Kuwaiti, and Palestinian friends. At times, Glenn would join. Soon Joyce and I began looking forward to these afternoon gatherings. Each time we offered them something to eat or drink, Mohammad and I would point with our heads at the ceramic plate hanging inside; smiling, he'd say "clin"; "clean," I'd reply.

It all seemed as simple as this: late summer; dizzying humidity; a shaded porch; a Jewish Turk, a Catholic Palestinian, Muslim men from Saudi Arabia and Kuwait, a Zen Buddhist and an American Catholic; on account of the heat, a dumb, defeated smile on everyone's face; the consolation of sameness; day after day, cool, clean lemonade.

Then the visits stopped suddenly on the day after the mosque massacre in Israel.

VII

Seferde is an Old Turkish word with Arabic roots, which means "on the journey." I don't think it has any etymological ties to the term, Sepharad, though it sounds alike and evokes the very soul of one of the most perpetual wanderings in Jewish history: an incomplete journey of men and women carrying memories of distant places and times.

For my Bar-Mitzva, I had to learn a passage about an early episode during the Exodus when Moses punishes one of the tribes for doubting God's plan. Father told me that the meaning of this passage was not the rehabilitation but the necessary sacrifice of the sceptics for the fulfillment of God's promise. I still remember the distinct terror that overtook me at the time. Where did I fit in this scheme of things? Where did we all fit in? Who could tell that our faith was strong enough to make it to the end of our journeys? Was the journey's end the sole proof of faith? Even then I had felt closer to Aaron than to Moses, the kind idol-builder who understood that faith involved many paths, many destinies, each fulfilling its own modest stretch on the way to God. Could this not be what God also knew all along since He envisioned that only the third generation of the wanderers, the unjaded, the undisappointed, would reach the Promised Land—when its promise finally looked achievable? If so, then God also understands the trails (trials?) of faith, the way it battles worldly circumstances, in which case the destiny assigned to the perpetual wanderer becomes an act of divine grace.

VIII

Don't forget the nut, being so proud of itself.
The body has its inward ways,
the five senses. They crack open,
and the Friend is revealed.
Crack open the Friend, you become
the All-One.
— Rumi

Leila wears her faith with quiet dignity among strangers. Except for her face and hands, she is entirely covered. Her head-piece is a tight, neatly wrapped scarf whose aura of restraint is overwhelmed by the deep, resonant green, orange, black and red stripes. Her face is framed by another scarf, white, silk, pinned under her chin. Her smile remains unperturbed, almost otherworldy. Whether she wears ornate vests or long, lacey shawls, she is always wrapped in vivid colors. Yet these remarkable clothes are not meant to make her stand out but stand in. Like prayer, her clothes define a singular space that deflect all voices and stares, and inside she is opened to the deep, peaceful silence through which God speaks.

140

IX

Dear Simone,

We had no choice but to leave; the distances that shape our lives have mapped the trajectory of mother's longing. Yet, we are still moving, which gives me hope. Somewhere, our life has entered its own course.

If we choose to remain anonymous in the cities we inhabit, it's beacuse we want their vastness. Space that can contain the memories of all places lost and still leave enough room for our hesitant feet to invent their walk.

I live in a small house with a garden, in the middle of this circle city. Practically from anywhere, I can view the open sky. I have roses and irises named after you, mother, father, grandparents, two old friends. I wait on them, learn them well. I made peace with the beetles that hound them in hot months. I receive accidental guests, keep the house ready for them, watch the young woman dressed in her piety walk our street. Like grandfather, I read the Torah, at times experiencing the serene silence that enveloped him in the reading. I take walks to the mosque to help my feet continue to remember. Everyday, I scrupulously count my blessings and losses.

Remember the pomegranates in the Song of Songs?

Don't write when you'll visit. Just come. As if returning.

United Methodist Church, **FLETCHER PLACE**

142

Meridian Street Episcopal Church, SANCTUARY, ERECTED 1905

143

United Methodist Church, FLETCHER PLACE

144

Meridian Street Methodist Church, ERECTED 1905

145

Meridian Street Methodist Church, ERECTED 1905

United Methodist Church, FLETCHER PLACE

146

United Methodist Church, **FLETCHER PLACE**

First United Brethren Church, **ERECTED 1921, DEMOLISHED 1997**

SPRING AT MOUNT ST. FRANCIS
Alice Friman

So much rain, even the dying
are fat, like this field of gold
dandelion gone to seed–God's hairs,
God's chest hairs–each
another universe on a launch pad,
another Big Bang ready to blow.

Dandelion as Absolute.
Plato's universal pattern.
Why not? When dandelions mature
the bracts ease back, letting the new
take over: petals laying themselves out
imitating suns, halos, crackers
around a cheese. Same as these
dead Franciscans laid out around
a center: a summons, a Christ.
Each holy life, a petal
shimmering under the grass.

Allergic to fluff or just plain
blind, but now I think I see. Look.
Spirits tend these graves, skinny things
with gray heads airy with space.
Virgin lightbulbs about to explode–
ghosts of that buried flower, risen
to start things over, shake loose and fly
whenever God, reading from His book,
yawns, and running a hand over His chest,
scratches inadvertently.

147

SACRED SPACE IN ORDINARY TIME
Susan Neville

"I'm beginning to feel the drunkenness that this agitated, tumultuous life plunges you into. With such a multitude of objects passing before my eyes, I'm getting dizzy. Of all the things that strike me, there is none that holds my heart, yet all of them together disturb my feelings, so that I forget what I am and who I belong to."
— *Rousseau, The New Eloise*

"Like a deer that longs for running streams, my soul longs for you my God. My soul is thirsting for the living God."
— *Psalm 42, excerpted from the liturgy, September 10, the 23rd Sunday in Ordinary Time*

Sunday, September 10, 1995. The 23rd Sunday of the year. It's the opening weekend of the Circle Centre Mall in Indianapolis, and the streets downtown are clotted with cars, the sidewalks with families, their faces tilted like rows of teacups toward the green glass of the Artsgarden and the elevated walkways. The glass is that lovely clear green of both pop bottles and a certain kind of volcanic rock. Not quite the fresh green of new leaves; this is a bluer green, inspiring a comfortable sun-lit awe, an all's-right-with-the-world awe, the awe you give to an always benevolent and easy-going God.

Isn't this a sacred space? All those steps leading up from the street like stairways to heaven! No matter what you might think you should feel about sacred structures, doesn't all this really feel sacred on this day? Did those old women and old men in their Sunday clothes emerging into the light from the darkness of their downtown mainstream churches have any more glorious an experience? None of this was here a few years ago and now, mysteriously, it's here right in front of you! These cathedrals of glass and stone!

Inside the mall there are young men standing on platforms with black virtual reality masks over their eyes and toy guns in their hands. They stand almost motionless except for a slight twitch in the arms or an almost invisible weaving of the body, though you know they feel themselves standing in a military landscape, their heads filled with loud cracks and ratcheting gunfire, with all the bright colors and geometric patterns of hallucination. The people sitting at tables and on benches watching them, in fact, remind you of the crowds you've read about, the ones that used to gather at the dockside to watch the "ships of fools" in medieval Europe–ships filled with psychotics who entertained the locals with their madness in the way that show boats used to bring theatre to towns along the Ohio River. But the entertainment level in the mall is a nice escape from all the objects, the glittering red bottles of cologne and the 200,000 shoes and the cast members in the Disney Store bemoaning that California has set their computer's clocks to "whatever time it is they think Indiana's on but isn't" and waiting to sing "Now it's time to say goodbye to all our company," to the shoppers at closing time. The mall was exciting in its way, but there was almost too much of it, and you for some reason felt this restless agitation you often feel when you spend too much time in a mall or in front of the television. You saw the same agitation in the children starting to whine and pull at their parents' hands, in the anxious lines of shoppers at the escalators. You realized that something is being desperately sought here and not quite being found.

According to the author of *Hoosier Faiths*, L.C. Rudolph, on any given weekend almost two million people in Indiana attend one of more than 10,000 places of worship. And still, theologians write, the most authentic religious experience in relation to sacred space, in modern times, is homesickness. The sense that we're cut off from something essential. That feeling that we've left something behind.

Outside, between the mall and the Pan Am Plaza and the RCA Dome, sits St. John's Catholic Church, designed by the architect D.A. Bohlen; it's been standing here since 1837. The exterior style is romanesque, early gothic, a simple brick with tall towers. The church is dwarfed by parking garages now and impossible to see if you're walking west on Georgia Street, and it emerges in your line of vision at the same time as the stadium, where the church is dwarfed by the stadium's dome, all white and billowing like a sheet on the line in the late-summer glare.

It's Sunday, and parking spaces are at a premium but the church's parking lot is empty. It's two hours after mass, but people respect the "church parking only" sign even on this day when downtown spaces are at a premium, and this is a prime location.

Inside St. John's, the altar is placed on the east side, as are the altars in European cathedrals, to catch the morning sun and to face Jerusalem.

But the large window above the altar in St. John's went dark when the parking garage next door was built, and now there's a perpetual spotlight on the garage's exterior to supply artificial sunlight and illuminate the figures in the colored glass so the parishioners can see them on Sunday morning.

All sacred space becomes, finally, almost by definition, contested space, space worth fighting for.

How can I explain how mysteriously beautiful the inside of St. John's is, skeptic that I am. It's impossible, William James would say; like all true experiences of the sacred, it's ineffable, beyond words. But the feeling resides in the architecture itself, and in the perpetual glittering of hundreds of red and gold and silver candles, bubbling like fireflies, each tiny flame representing a departed soul that someone living wants remembered. And in the mystery of the priest buried in the floor of the church, who was born in France in 1815, and died in Indianapolis, a pioneer, "in the hope of a blessed immortality." The stained glass windows are deep blood red and cobalt blue, and statues and altars line the walls.

What makes architectural space sacred? When I drove through Batesville a few weeks ago, there was a white frame church with beautiful stained glass windows and a Talk to Tucker sign in the front yard. There's another beautiful old church for sale on Highway 31 North, near South Bend, stained glass still intact on the first and second floors, plywood covering the circular hole in the bell tower where a window once was, like a patch on an eye gone dark. When the insurance company or real estate agency that buys it moves in, will these buildings continue to be sacred? At what precise moment will they stop being so, or have they already been profaned by the sign itself? Or were they profaned earlier, when the human beings who built them stopped honoring the place with their rituals?

In Indiana, sacred space seems to be fluid like this, and our sacred places are almost exclusively architectural. Maybe it's because this is a landscape that's been changed so completely by human hands. And the natural features, the dense forests and swampland that might have resonated with non-human power, have been erased. In Greece, for instance, you can tell when you're near-

149

ing the temple of a god because of the feeling that's engendered by the landscape, the particular view of the ocean or mountains letting you know that you've arrived.

But architecture plays chords of feeling as well. It's lyrical and, like lyrical poetry, it exists to praise something in particular. It engenders feeling because it begins with feeling. A particular type of building causes particular emotional strings to resonate, and as long as that building stands, it will continue to play its own particular music in the human heart. And it's an art that both captures space for a particular use and serves as a living historical document.

I suppose that one question you need to answer when trying to define sacred space is the question Frost asks about fences. What are you walling in or walling out? In the case of the mall, what's being celebrated is the marketplace, and the feeling is an agitated desire to buy. The history that's recorded in its style is late twentieth century post-modernism. Past styles are alluded to in fragments—in the facades of storefronts and in the old Ayres clock—but it's all pastiche, a mask, a borrowing from different styles and different times, covering what is in fact a shell of the standard Nordstrom's.

In the case of a church or synagogue or mound or mosque, the feeling is mystery and awe and grandeur and faith, something invisible, like a ghost, that some group of people at one time or another thought important enough to throw a sheet over, a sheet made of stone and glass and earth, to show that it was there. It may not rise from the landscape itself in Indiana, but from the human heart. This is why even a space that began as secular space can evoke those same feelings of mystery, why preservationists fight for some space as though it's sacred. Because in the midst of its decay, it's grown into its true nature. It's like a bowl that's been emptied and refilled with

mystery: so this is human striving, what it comes to in the end. A sense of the sacred, those truths that, unchanging, are at the very ground of being.

Simone Weil thought that to really fix your attention is to pray. And so this essay, intended to celebrate the wealth of sacred space in Indianapolis from Second Presbyterian to the Jewish/Catholic cemeteries on Indianapolis's southside. These outward manifestations of something invisible, the historical record of the spiritual life of generations.

◆ ◆ ◆

Sunday morning in Indianapolis, ordinary times. I decide to go to as many sacred places as I can in one day, to as many church services and burial grounds, to try and hear what's being said in this once-a-week murmuring beneath the clamor of dailiness. All day long I have the same experience everywhere I go. I see people I haven't seen in years: my cousin's mother-in-law, my fifth-grade teacher, retired professors from Butler, second and third cousins, grade-school friends with their now grade-school-aged children. So this, I think, is where you've all been hiding.

At the Spiritualist Church in Broad Ripple, ten minutes before the healing service, a woman in knit pants and T-shirt bends over to pick a weed out out of the garden. At the Baptist Church, elderly women with pastel blouses talk in the parking lot. In the sun, their hair is fiery white as the floodlights on the altar. Model T drivers are driving their Model Ts in a row along Kessler Boulevard; young couples with infants walk in and out of the bagel shop. All of them celebrating the morning sun, the sky a blue ether that goes on for miles.

In the Gothic Second Presbyterian Church the early service is in the chapel, and it's packed. The men wear jackets even on this hot summer day, and the women are chips of stained glass in

150

red and turquoise linen. Someone's watch beeps the time as the minister gives his sermon. "The cybernetic revolution has come," he says, "like a thief in the night." "Our creator," he explains, "has given us a choice to program computers of our souls to bless him or curse him."

At the Allisonville Christian Church they're saying good-bye to the old sanctuary and blessing the new one. For months workers have built the new sanctuary, hammering, glazing windows, placing the new steeple. The new roof blazes copper. The old sanctuary is blue, like water, and without the pews and the flowers smell musty. "We give thanks," the minister says as he walks up from the old space to the new, "for dreams that harden into steel and stone and mortar."

The point of the sermons at the conservative Reverend Greg Dixon's Baptist Temple (where you can buy How and Why to Form Your Own Militia pamphlets in the lobby) and the liberal All Souls Unitarian (You can be a Christian Unitarian, someone explains to me, or a Buddhist Unitarian, or an Emersonian Unitarian, or even a pagan Unitarian) are strangely similar. This is a time of group think, we're told, and this sacred place is one of the last bastions of free thought. The style of the sermons is different, of course, the syntax and word choice, the examples, the intonation. But the message, on this day, is the same. You could attribute it to synchronicity, to the collective unconscious. But I decide that it's because both Baptists and Unitarians love ideas, albeit different ones, and they both have a deep wish for utopian perfectability somewhere out there in the future, albeit different utopias and different futures.

The first Protestant church in Indiana, in fact, was a Baptist church. And what was appealing to pioneers about the Baptist faith was its sense of independence. Since there was no direct authority,

no human authority, beyond the word of God, settlers could "personally use the Bible as a direct guide to reconstitute the pure apostolic church at any time or place." For the nondoctrinaire Unitarian, there is no authority beyond the individual's own most quiet inner voice.

Tell your stories, a former minister, HIV positive, says to a congregation of men and women with AIDS. Your stories are sacred. Make people call you by name.

This process, he says, going through hell and coming out the other side, has a name as well. It's resurrection. To love another person is to see the face of God.

At the downtown Spiritualist church, there's a small gathering. I imagine what it must have been like in the late nineteenth century when there was that resurgence of interest in the occult, in the belief in a permeable door between the world of the living and the world of the dead.

Camp Chesterfield, north of Indianapolis, was founded in 1888, and New Harmony's Robert Dale Owen published his autobiography, *Threading My Way*, in which he recounts his conversion to Spiritualism, in 1874. In 1883, in Indianapolis, Booth Tarkington's sister, Haute, discovered she had a gift for levitating tables, a gift that disappeared, along with her singing voice, when she married.

For fifteen minutes there's a brief service with old-fashioned hymns and a sermon. On the altar, there are white candles in tall glasses like milk. "In the name of Christ," a woman prays, "we come to you for healing."

After this, the unusual part of the service begins. The three mediums give their messages to each member in the congregation. "As I come to you I'm seeing: daisies, gilted, almost an artificial look; a syringe, a Bavarian building with cobblestones, white baked bread, a pinwheel off center." Mediums are poets, I realize, and they deliver their messages from the dead in the language of metaphor.

I drive south of the city to the Jewish Cemetery, space purchased by the Indianapolis Hebrew Congregation in 1858 for $125. Until 1824, "not a single congregation (of Jews) existed within 500 miles of Cincinnati." But by 1859 there was a population of 3000 Jews in Indiana, primarily spurred by German and then Eastern European migration. The cemetery's stones are close together, and in front of each stone there's something like the foundation of a house bordering the plot. And within the foundation, piles of other stones commemorating the life of the dead.

The feeling here is of something singular, solid and everlasting as granite. Unlike flowers, stones endure, they're bedrock, and when a mourner brings one stone and places it by or on top of another there's a community of mourners stretching across space and back through time.

Next to the Jewish cemetery is St. Joseph's Catholic cemetery. You drive in the front gate off of Meridian thinking nothing much different here, no stones shaped like tree trunks or doll houses, no stones leaning one way from military target practice, as there are in Bartholomew County.

But then you reach the top of the hill and make a right and, like the Jewish cemetery, you're once again in a world of stone, the fluid universe all hardened and fixed. Both cemeteries are almost terrifyingly holy. This is death. This is what you can count on. A sign tells us that this is "a resting place until the day of resurrection for the bodies. . . once temples of the holy spirit whose souls are now with God."

The stones here are tall with thick pale crosses, and you get a sense of movement, strangely, the white rock crosses on the top of the monuments like a large flock of birds taking off at once, with you standing in the center of it. And at your feet, row after row of nineteenth-century nuns and priests.

◆ ◆ ◆

The last thing I do is look for a storefront church I used to drive by on my way to work.

But they've torn down the wall between Marty's New and Used Furniture and Ebenezer Gospel Ministries, and Marty's daughter tries to tell me why. "They only had ten or twelve people anyway, never paid their rent, never paid the utilities. They'd stay in here all night and then hide out or leave when we came in the day. So we had them evicted, locked them out, the whole thing.

"It wasn't a real faith anyway," she says, "not a real church.

"It was a ranting and raving full Gospel holy roller thing. Not any kind of faith."

This had been an urban block with two storefront charismatic churches and several junk shops. At night, for over a year, you could drive by at night and the junk shops would be dark and murky and there in the middle of block, in the one rectangle of light, a woman in a long white robe would weave and wave her arms and you could watch young men and women jump up and swoon and shout in their plain white shirts and black pants or skirts—the universal uniform of school choirs. They were the initiates, the family, a community of ecstatics.

And the whole block except for that light would disappear, all the cast-off man-made objects of this world and their embarrassing decay—the fraying fabrics and hideous shapes, the colors that we loved once and grew to hate through familiarity and the need for change; they were nothing but old husks, old bodies. Someone, somewhere, felt well rid of them.

But across the street, I see, there's another storefront

152

church. And two more a block over. And a center for Islam. Sacred space disappearing and reappearing, the spirit in the buildings, windows burning and extinguished and burning again, like flickering candles.

Throughout cities, there's this countermovement, this undertow to the story of the mall and St. John's. When Marty's New and Used moves out, as landlords abandon buildings or accept smaller and smaller rent checks, Ebenezer's Gospel Ministries or some sister church will probably move back in, and the block, and many like it, become a sanctification of space, a resurrection of stuff. And this, I think, is the story of Indiana's sacred places, the sacred fighting for its place in a world of civil government and commerce, re-emerging over and over in all its diversity, its multitude of eclectic styles.

"The Miracles of the Church," Willa Cather wrote, "seem to me to rest not so much upon faces or voices or healing power but upon our perception being made finer, so that coming suddenly near us from afar off, for a moment our eyes can see and our ears can hear what there is about us always." On the way home, I drive by A More Excellent Way Outreach Ministries: Holy Ghost and Fire. It shares half of a building with the Soul Food Cafe, a fiery dove painted on a window next to a painted, steaming cup of coffee, the steam and dove rising, simultaneously, into the blue air.

WHAT COUNTS

Yusef Komunyakaa

I thumb pages, thinking onion
or shreds of garlic
flicked into my eyes.
Maybe the light's old,
or the earth begs every drop
of water it dares to caress.
I leaf through the anthology,
almost unconscious, unaware
I'm counting the dead faces
I've known. Two Roberts—
Hayden & Duncan. Dick
Hugo. Bill Stafford &
Nemerov. Here's Etheridge's
"Circling the Daughter"
again, basic as a stone
dropped into a creek,
a voice fanning out
circles on delta nights.
Anne's haze-eyed blues
at dusk in a bestiary
behind her "reference
work in sin." If we were
ever in the same room,
it isn't for the living
to figure out. Unearthly

desire makes man & woman
God's celestial wishbone
to snap at midnight. Pages
turn on their own & I listen:
Son, be careful what you
wish for. Do I want my name
here, like x's in the eyes
of ex-lovers? I'm thankful
for the cities we drank
wine & talked about swing
bands from Kansas City
into the after hours
under green weather
in this age of reason.

ANODYNE

Yusef Komunyakaa

I love how it swells
into a temple where it is
held prisoner, where the god
of blame resides. I love
slopes & peaks, the secret
paths that make me selfish.
I love my crooked feet
shaped by vanity & work
shoes made to outlast
belief. The hardness
coupling milk it can't
fashion. I love the lips,
salt & honeycomb on the tongue.
The hair holding off rain
& snow. The white moons
on my fingernails. I love
how everything begs
blood into song & prayer
inside an egg. A ghost
hums through my bones
like Pan's midnight flute
shaping internal laws
beside a troubled river.
I love this body
made to weather the storm

in the brain, raised
out of the deep smell
of fish & water hyacinth,
out of rapture & the first
regret. I love my big hands.
I love it clear down to the soft
quick motor of each breath,
the liver's ten kinds of desire
& the kidney's lust for sugar.
This skin, this sac of dung
& joy, this spleen floating
like a compass needle inside
nighttime, always divining
West Africa's dusty horizon.
I love the birthmark
posed like a fighting cock
on my right shoulder blade.
I love this body, this
solo & ragtime jubilee
behind the left nipple,
because I know I was born
to wear out at least
one hundred angels.

CONTRIBUTORS
Writers

ARON R. AJI is an associate professor of Comparative Literature at Butler University. He has edited *Milan Kundera and the Art of Fiction*, authored papers on Kundera, Rushdie, Achebe, Soyinka, and translated the works of the Turkish author, Bilge Karasu. He teaches courses on European, Islamic, and African literatures, and studies, on his own, the Torah and Jewish mystical texts.

MARIANNE BORUCH teaches in the MFA program at Purdue University, and recent poetry has appeared in *APR, Pequod, Georgia Review, Iowa Review*, and elsewhere. She is the author of four poetry collections, the most recent, *A Stick that Breaks and Breaks* (Oberlin College Press, 1997) and the essay collection *Poetry's Old Air* (University of Michigan Press, 1995).

NANCY NIBLACK BAXTER is the president of Guild Press of Indiana and author of numerous books, including the historical novels *The Movers, Lords of the Rivers, The Dream Divided, All the Bright Sons of Morning*, and *Charmed Circle*. She is also the author of *Hoosier Farmboy in Lincoln's Army, Gallant Fourteenth: The Story of an Indiana Civil War Regiment*, and *The Miamis!*

J. KENT CALDER is managing editor for the Indiana Historical Society and editor of the society's illustrated magazine, *Traces of Indiana and Midwestern History*. His articles and reviews have appeared in *Arts Indiana, The Journal of Scholarly Publishing, Documentary Editing*, and *Indiana Magazine of History*.

DAN CARPENTER is an Indianapolis native and a copy editor and writer for the *Indianapolis Star*. He's contributed fiction to several journals and published a collection of his newspaper columns in the book *Hard Pieces* (Indiana University Press, 1993).

ALICE FRIMAN, born in New York City, has lived in Indianapolis since 1960. The author of *Reporting from Corinth, Inverted Fire*, and four chapbooks, she is the winner of the Award for Excellence in Poetry from *Hopewell Review*, 1995, Japan's Abiko Quarterly

International Poetry Contest, 1994, and three prizes from Poetry Society of America. Her poems have appeared in *Poetry, Georgia Review, Gettysburg Review, Shenandoah, Manoa,* and publications in seven other countries.

PATRICIA HENLEY grew up in Vigo County near the Old Paris Road. Graywolf Press published two collections of her short stories, *Friday Night at Silver Star* (1985) and *The Secret of Cartwheels* (1993). She lives in Battle Ground, Indiana, and since 1987 has taught in the Creative Writing Program at Purdue University.

DAVID HOPPE is a freelance writer and editor whose articles have appeared in many journals, including, *Traces of Indiana and Midwestern History, Exquisite Corpse, Arts Indiana, New Art Examiner,* and *NUVO.* He is the editor of *Hard Pieces: Selected Writings by Dan Carpenter* (Indiana University Press, 1993) and *Where We Live: Essays about Indiana* (Indiana University Press, 1989).

ETHERIDGE KNIGHT is an award-winning poet who died on March 10, 1990. His writings include *Poems from Prison* (1968), *Belly Song and other Poems* (1973), and *Born of Woman* (1980). He lived much of his life in Indianapolis, received fellowships from the National Endowment for the Arts and the Guggenheim Foundation, and was awarded the Shelley Memorial Award from the Poetry Society of America in 1985.

YUSEF KOMUNYAKAA is the author of nine books, including *Magic City, Thieves of Paradise,* and the Pulitzer Prize-winning *Neon Vernacular,* (1993). He taught at Indiana University in Bloomington for many years and is currently teaching at Princeton.

ANDREW LEVY is an associate professor of English at Butler University. He is the author of *The Culture and Commerce of the American Short Story*, co-author of *Creating Fiction*, and co-editor of *Postmodern American Fiction, A Norton Anthology.*

MICHAEL MARTONE was born and raised in Fort Wayne, Indiana. He attended Butler University and graduated from Indiana University, Bloomington. He has published five books of fiction set in Indiana. *Seeing Eye,* the most recent, was published by Zoland Books in 1995. He now lives in Tuscaloosa, Alabama.

ALYCE MILLER's book *The Nature of Longing,* won the 1993 Flannery O'Connor Award, and was republished in paperback by W. W. Norton. Her novel, *Stopping for Green Lights,* is forthcoming this year from Anchor Doubleday. Her short fiction has appeared in numerous journals and has won such awards as the Kenyon Review Award of Literary Excellence in Fiction and the Lawrence Foundation Prize. She also publishes poetry and essays. She left San Francisco in 1995 to join the MFA faculty at Indiana University in Bloomington.

SUSAN NEVILLE is Demia Butler Professor of English at Butler University. Her most recent collection of stories, *In the House of Blue Lights,* won the Richard Sullivan Fiction Prize from Notre Dame. She is also the author of *Indiana Winter,* a collection of essays, and the story collection *The Invention of Flight.* She wishes to acknowledge the proofreading skills of Greg Pearson.

JIM POYSER is Arts & Entertainment Editor of the *Bloomington Voice,* and Fine Arts Editor of *NUVO Newsweekly.* He lives in Indianapolis and writes plays, screenplays, fiction, and haiku.

SCOTT RUSSELL SANDERS is a professor of English at Indiana University, Bloomington. His books include *Hunting for Hope, Staying Put, The Paradise of Bombs,* and *Writing from the Center* (Indiana University Press, 1995). His work has been selected for the Associated Writing Programs Award in Creative Nonfiction, the Ohioiana Book Award, Best American Essays, the Kenyon Review Award for Literary Excellence, and the Lannon Literary Award.

SANDY EISENBERG SASSO is Rabbi at Congregation Beth-El Zedeck in Indianapolis and lectures at Christian Theological Seminary and Butler University. She is the author of many articles and of five children's books dealing with the issues of spirituality. Two of her books *But God Remembered* and *A Prayer for the Earth* were selected as best books of the year by *Publisher's Weekly.*

BARBARA SHOUP is the author of three novels: *Night Watch, Wish You Were Here,* and *Stranded in Harmony.* Her short fiction, poetry, essays, and interviews have appeared in *Mississippi Valley Review, Crazy Quilt, Louisville Review, The Journal of the Jane Austin Society of North America, Rhino, The New York Times Travel Section,* and other magazines. She has been the writer-in-residence at Broad Ripple High School Center for the Humanities since 1982.

Recently retired, BERT STERN is Milligan Professor of English, Emeritus, at Wabash College. He is the author of a book on Wallace Stevens, and his essays and poems have appeared in *New Republic, The American Poetry Review, Sewanee Review, Columbia Teachers College Record, Poetry, Southern Review,* and elsewhere.

JEANETTE VANAUSDALL is a freelance writer and editor. She recently completed a book about the novel in Indiana, to be published by the Indiana Historical Society in 1999.

DAN WAKEFIELD's credits as a journalist, screenwriter, and author include the bestselling novels *Starting Over* and *Going All the Way* and the memoirs *New York in the Fifties* and *Returning.* Indiana University Press published a new edition of his novel *Going All the Way* to coincide with the release of the motion picture in 1997.

STEPHEN H. WEBB is an associate professor of Religion and Philosophy at Wabash College, Crawfordsville, Indiana. He is the author of many articles and four books, most recently, *On God and Dogs: A Christian Theology of Compassion for Animals,* published by Oxford University Press.

157

Photographers

KIM CHARLES FERRILL is a freelance photographer who works with the Indiana Historical Society. He has illustrated the books *Hoosier Faiths* (Indiana University Press, 1995), *Where God's People Meet* (Guild Press, 1996), *Voices of Faith* for The Polis Center, and is currently working on *Sacred Heartland,* a book funded by a Clio grant from the Indiana Historical Society. Ferrill's photographs seek to show the human quality that is reflected in all religious structures. He wishes to acknowledge the invaluable help of Joan E. Hostetler in editing the photographs for this collection.

DARRYL JONES is a freelance photographer. His books include *Indiana, Indiana II, Owen Sweet Owen, Indianapolis,* and *The Spirit of the Place.* Jones's photographs of the Joy of All Who Sorrow Eastern Orthodox Church show a community of spiritual involvement. Largely American converts, the parishioners value the hidden treasure of Holy Orthodoxy, reflected in the fullness of celebration of the church feasts and services and through missionary outreach to the greater community of Indianapolis.

TYAGAN MILLER is a documentary and commercial photographer. His photographic projects include "High Risk: Students of the IPS Alternative Schools, 1992-1996" and "Being Old: The Lives of Our Elders." For this project Miller photographed the life of Friendship Missionary Baptist Church. To do so, he attended nearly a year of Sunday services. The church's covenant provided him with a frame in which to work. The covenant charges members of the congregation to participate in the life of the church in three ways: through Christ-like interactions with one another and with nonmembers, through regular study of the Bible, and through devotions.

CARL POPE's photographs and mixed media works have been widely exhibited and are in the permanent collections of the Museum of Modern Art in New York, the Whitney Museum of Art, and the Indianapolis Museum of Art. He has received fellowships from the National Endowment for the Arts and the John Simon Guggenheim Memorial Foundation. Pope's photographs for this project were taken at events where the spiritual connection of the Islamic community shows a common bond of faith, love, and commitment that transcends the boundaries of race, class, ethnicity, and national origin.

GINNY TAYLOR ROSNER's current work features abandoned spaces. She is active with Testimony Ministries, Inc., a ministry of Christian artists, and teaches art at the Plainfield Juvenile Correctional Facility. Her photographs were included in the group show, Nine for the Nineties in 1991 at the Indianapolis Museum of Art. Rosner's images of abandoned sacred structures reveal her search for the "presence" that transcends the ordinary within the context of abandoned settings.

JEFFREY A. WOLIN is Professor of Photography and Director of the School of Fine Arts at Indiana University. He has received two fellowships from the National Endowment for the Arts and a John Simon Guggenheim Memorial Fellowship. His series of portraits of Holocaust survivors, *Written in Memory: Portraits of the Holocaust,* was publish by Chronicle Books in 1997. He has exhibited widely, and his work is in the permanent collections of the Museum of Contemporary Art in Chicago, the Center for Creative Photography in Tucson, and the George Eastman House. Wolin's contribution to this project shows the wide range of belief and practice within the contemporary Jewish community of Indianapolis.